Learn Spanish Easy Guide

Best Easy Guide, Practicing Grammar and Conversation in Spanish Language!

Anthony García

Table of Contents

INTRODUCTION 7
- A. METHOD OF LEARNING A NEW LANGUAGE 8
- B. THE SPANISH LANGUAGE 9
- C. HOW TO PRONOUNCE THE VOWELS 10
- D. PRONUNCIATION 11
- E. WHERE TO GO FROM HERE 16
- F. THE STRESS RULES 17

VOCABULARY IN EATING OUT 19
- THE FOOD CULTURE IN SPAIN 19
- SPANISH EATING HABITS AND MANNERS 19
- TRADITIONAL SPANISH YOU SHOULDN'T MISS 21
- MUST-KNOW SPANISH FOOD VOCABULARY 24
- WORDS AND PHRASES YOU SHOULD KNOW WHEN DINING IN A RESTAURANT 33
- TIPS FOR PROPER SPANISH ETIQUETTE FOR DINING 37

ASKING FOR DIRECTIONS 40
- DON'T BE AFRAID TO ASK 40
- USING ADDRESSES 41
- KNOW YOUR DIRECTIONS 42
- ADDITIONAL DIRECTIONS AND SAMPLE CONVERSATIONS 50
- TWO TIPS FOR CONVERSATION WHEN ASKING FOR DIRECTIONS 52

TRAVELING BY BUS & TRAIN 54
- TRAVELING IN SPAIN 54
- MEANS OF TRANSPORTATION IN SPAIN 55
- IMPORTANT BASIC TRANSPORTATION VOCABULARY AND PHRASES IN SPANISH 56
- TRAVELING BY TRAIN IN SPANISH-SPEAKING COUNTRIES 60
- TRAVELING BY BUS IN SPANISH-SPEAKING COUNTRIES 63
- TIPS FOR TRAVELLING BY BUS, TRAIN, AND OTHER PUBLIC TRANSPORTATIONS IN SPAIN 66

INTRODUCING & TALKING ABOUT YOURSELF 68

GETTING STARTED: BASIC VOCABULARY AND PHRASES INTRODUCE
YOURSELF IN SPANISH 68
STEP-BY-STEP METHOD TO INTRODUCE YOURSELF IN SPANISH 71
OTHER METHODS TO INTRODUCE YOURSELF IN SPANISH 72

USEFUL PHRASES WHEN SHOPPING 78

SHOP LIKE A BOSS IN SPANISH – WHY IS IT IMPORTANT? 78
ESSENTIAL SPANISH WORDS AND PHRASES TO BECOME A SAVVY
SHOPPER 80
HOW TO BARGAIN SMARTLY 89

VOCABULARY FOR CONVERSING WITH A PHARMACIST
OR DOCTOR 93

COMMON MEDICAL SPANISH PHRASES YOU CAN USE AND HEAR AT
THE DOCTOR'S OFFICE 93
SPANISH MEDICAL PHRASES DOCTORS USE WHEN ASKING ABOUT
SYMPTOMS 95
SPANISH MEDICAL PHRASES TO USE AT THE PHARMACY 96

LEARN TO DEAL WITH BUSINESS SITUATIONS AND
DISCUSS THE WEATHER 101

SPANISH PHRASES TO USE IN BUSINESS SITUATIONS 101
SPANISH WEATHER VOCABULARY 103

PRACTICE & REVISION OF YOUR SPANISH
VOCABULARY 108

START BY PRACTICING AND HONING YOUR SPANISH GRAMMAR 108
PAY ATTENTION TO YOUR PRONUNCIATION 110
PRACTICE YOUR VOCABULARY 111

CONCLUSION 114

(CONCLUSIÓN) 114

© Copyright 2021 by Anthony García - All rights reserved. The following Book is reproduced below with the goal of providing information that is as accurate and reliable as possible. Regardless, purchasing this Book can be seen as consent to the fact that both the publisher and the author of this book are in no way experts on the topics discussed within and that any recommendations or suggestions that are made herein are for entertainment purposes only. Professionals should be consulted as needed prior to undertaking any of the action endorsed here in. This declaration is deemed fair and valid by both the American Bar Association and the Committee of Publishers Association and is legally binding throughout the United States. Furthermore, the transmission, duplication, or reproduction of any of the following work including specific information will be considered an illegal act irrespective of if it is done electronically or in print. This extends to creating a secondary or tertiary copy of the work or a recorded copy and is only allowed with the express written consent from the Publisher. All additional right reserved.

The information in the following pages is broadly considered a truthful and accurate account of facts and as such, any inattention, use, or misuse of the information in question by the reader will render any resulting actions solely under their purview. There are no scenarios in which the publisher or the original author of this work can be in any fashion deemed liable for any hardship or damages that may befall them after undertaking information described herein.

Additionally, the information in the following pages is intended only for informational purposes and should thus be thought of as universal. As befitting its nature, it is presented without assurance regarding its prolonged validity or interim quality. Trademarks that are mentioned are done without written consent and can in no way be considered an endorsement from the trademark holder.

Introduction

Are you one of those people who have been considering learning a new language? Is Spanish the one you are considering to learn? In case you didn't know yet, Spanish is one of the most widely spoken languages in the world. More than five hundred million individuals are native Spanish speakers. Therefore, by that figure, it is considered as the second most sought-after language following Mandarin Chinese. Apart from that, a study has shown that it's the most romantic of all languages. No matter if you wish to learn the language simply to widen your knowledge or you simply want to learn it because you're traveling a Spanish-speaking destination, you will require a guide to make your whole learning process much simpler and stress-free.

This book is suitable for you, especially if you're not trying to pass a Spanish class. That's because it will get you speaking the language quick. In any scenario, you don't need to be a language professor just to speak the language. This book will surely teach you how to speak the language with the help of simple and practical examples. It will also walk you through discussions to help you get your point across whenever you are meeting new individuals, finding directions, going shopping, traveling, eating in a restaurant, and so much more. In short, this book will guide you on how to speak Spanish virtually in any sort of situation.

The good thing here is that you won't find boring grammar lessons and rules you wouldn't bother with anyway. As an alternative, you will explore many practical examples as well as notes, which will guide you on how to understand better how to speak. While the Spanish language isn't as complex to learn as English is, the language does have its quirks, you must be familiar.

You will find many reasons for desiring to learn the Spanish language. First, because being bilanguage will make you desirable in the job marketplace. It will also provide you a higher sense of self-confidence if you could step in and assist individuals who are having a difficult time with the language barrier out in public. Have you ever thought of how many instances you've seen somebody speaking the language and having trouble to communicate with other people? You wish you could help them but you can't. Today, you don't need just to stand there. You could finally step in and help both people.

Learning a new language like Spanish is advantageous to your self-value and resume as well. What's more, it is a wonderful way to keep your brain exercising. Some people don't stop learning. Therefore, learning a new language could be your initial step to continuing education.

As you now go on along with the learning journey, you'll discover different vital tips, which make will understanding and speaking the language much simple. Using this book, you could be talking Spanish in no time at all. Best of luck and buen viaje!

A. Method of Learning a New Language

Efficient language learners have a positive response when faced with the unfamiliar. Therefore, instead of letting yourself to feel pissed, confused, and frustrated every time listening to Spanish, why don't you try to keep a positive point of view? Start working to know anything you could. It could help you think of speaking in Spanish as a puzzle to be solved, or it could be an interesting challenge to be reached. Every time you hear spoken Spanish, you must concentrate on what is being told. Do not get distracted by your negative ideas. Listen for cognates that are words, which are similar or almost the same in two languages. Take note that English and Spanish share many cognates. Some of these are much

/ **mucho**; culture / **cultura**; aspect / **aspecto**; important / **importante**; professor / **professor**; introductory / **introductorio**; and course / **curso**.

B. The Spanish Language

The Spanish language is also called as **castellano** or **español.** This language was established in the Iberian Peninsula in the region of Castile. Spanish is considered as the third most spoken language in the world, according to the United Nations. Approximately, at least half a billion of folks speak the language. It is spoken on four continents and is the official language of twenty nations.

Aside from that, the language is also spoken more every year in the mainland of the U.S. In fact, approximately forty million individuals in the U.S. speak the language at home. That makes up over twelve percent of the population of the country. A 2015 report conducted by a government organization in Spain sowed that there are more Spanish speakers in the U.S. compared there to Spain. You will find three major differences, which determine how this language is spoken in one region versus another. This includes grammar, accent, and vocabulary. The differences in vocabulary lead in various words utilized in various locations to refer to a similar thing. For instance, the word "the computer" in Latin America is **la computadora**. Meanwhile, you will say it in Spain as **el ordenador**.

When we talk about the accent, you will find some variances among regions. You will also find differences between regions in a similar country. The most evident difference in accent among those Spanish speaker connects to the way to say the letter **z**, the letter **c** then followed by **e** or **i**.

Another example is in Latin America, the letter **z, as well as the letter,** mixes **ci** and **ce** are spoken along with an **s** sound. On the other hand, in central and northern Spain, it was spoken along with **th** sound. For instance, the term for "shoe" is **zapato**. In Latin America, it is uttered as **sapato.** In Madrid, it is spoken as **thapato.**

You might not notice many grammatical differences among regions. However, there are some, which deal with the plural form of "you." In both Latin America and Spain, the term **ustedes** is the formal and plural way to talk "you." Meanwhile in Spain, you will find an informal and plural way to utter "you." **Vosotras** in the feminine while **vosotros** in the masculine. However, **vosotras** and **vosotros** aren't utilized in Latin America. As an alternative, **ustedes** is utilized for the plural "you" in every scenario. Regardless of such differences in grammar, accent as well as vocabulary, thousands of Spanish speakers converse efficiently across every region where the language is pronounced. Even those speakers of Spanish from various countries understand one another totally well.

C. How to Pronounce the Vowels

Speaking words in Spanish is easier than it is in the English language. That's mainly because if you see a letter in Spanish, you will understand how to speak the sound of that particular letter. The only difficult part of the pronunciation of the Spanish language is that you will find sounds in the language, which do not exist, in the English language. All of them could be hard to speak at first. Every vowel – **a, e, i, o, u** – make only one sound in Spanish. It is only a quick sound, which remains the same from start to finish, Here's a detailed example:
- The vowel **A** seen in the typical Spanish term **casa** is the simplest vowel sound to create. The other four vowel

sounds concentrate on maintaining the vowel sound brief and constant.
- The vowel **E** creates the sound spoken in the English word "t<u>a</u>ke." You see, it is not pronounced "eyyyy." You do not end it off at the end as we mostly do in the English language.
- The vowel **I** create the sound spoken in the word "f<u>ee</u>." It is not "iyyy."
- The vowel **B** creates the sound spoken in "t<u>oi</u>l." It is not "owww."
- The vowel **U** creates the sound spoken in "r<u>u</u>le." It is not "uwww."

D. Pronunciation

Pronunciation is vital in any type of language. Therefore, get the hang of this before you try to talk to someone. Nowadays, it is much simpler, simply because you will find countless videos online that will aid you. In this section, you will learn how to utter individual letters by fitting them into typical, easily spoken Spanish words.
One benefits of Spanish over the English language is that with the majority of words, the pronunciation is phonetic. You see, the words sound as if they're spelled. You will also find some homophones that will puzzle you. Some of those words include "they're," "their," and "there" that sound the same; however, have different spellings and meanings. Below is a brief guide to Spanish pronunciation.

The Vowels
In the Spanish language, you will find five vowels and one sound for every vowel.

[a]	ah	The 'a' is spoken as if you were gargling. Simply open your mouth wide and say as saw and father. Try **mapa, agua.**
[e]	eh	The 'e' sound isn't totally existent in English. The nearest pronunciation might be 'eh' as red and met. You must not say the 'e' as in English. You can try saying **enero, verde.**
[i]	ee	The 'i' sound is somewhat similar to 'ee' as bee and feet. You see, the 'i' sound is much different compared to the English pronunciation. For instance, **mi, fino.**
[o]	oh	The letter 'o' is uttered as 'oh.' However, it has a shorter sound as know and boat. You can try **roto, coco.**
[u]	oo	This is pronounced as 'oo' like in do or boot. Try saying **muro, futuro.**

The Diphthongs

In case you didn't know yet, a diphthong is a sound that was made by a mix of two (2) vowels in a single syllable. A sound starts as one vowel and moves to another.

|a|+|i|	ai, ay	The 'ai' and 'ay' sound is like ay and why. You can try speaking **mayo, aire.**
|a|+|u|	au	The 'au' sounds like the expression auch. You can try speaking **aula, aunque.**
|e|+|u|	eu	You will not find a sound for this in the English language. That was something like ew however, with the use of the 'e' sound as bed and the 'u' as do. You can try saying **deudor, Europa.**

	e	+	i		ey, ei	The pronunciation of 'ey' and ei' is near to say and hey. Try saying **buy, reina.**
	i	+	a		ia	The 'ia' will sounds like tiara and yah. Try saying **anciano, piano.**
	i	+	e		ie	The 'ie' sounds similar to yes. Try saying **fiera, tierra.**
	i	+	o		io	The 'io' is uttered as John or yo-yo. Try saying **rio, radio.**
	i	+	u		iu	The 'iu' is uttered as you. You can try saying **viuda, ciudad.**
	o	+	i		oy, oi	The 'oy' and 'oi' sounds similar to boy and toy. Try saying **heroico, hoy.**
	u	+	a	ua	The 'ua' sound is similar to water. You can try saying **aduana, actuar.**
	u	+	e		ue	The 'ue' sounds similar to wet. Try saying **sueño** and **Huevo.**
u	+	i		ui	The 'ui' sounds is similar to wheat and we. Try saying **huir, arruinar.**
	u	+	o		uo	The 'uo' sounds similar to continuous and quote. Try saying **cuota, individuo.**

The Consonants

A series of Spanish consonants are pronounced differently from their English counterparts. If you could, you can try to listen to a local speaker and hear how they deal with them.

| [b] | Beh | The letter 'b' is uttered after n, m, or l. The sound of this letter is similar to bear and Venice, even though the lips should not touch. For example, **bonito.** |
| [c] | Ceh | The letter 'c' sounds like cereal before i or e. Or else, it might sound like 'k' as computer. |

		For example, **computadora** as 'k' and **cereza** as 'c.'
[ch]	Cheh	For example, **chico, chocolate.**
[d]	Deh	For example, **dos, dust.**
[f]	Effe	The letter 'f" sounds similar in the English fountain or Eiffel. For example, **familia.**
[g]	Heh	The 'g' sounds is similar to her before i or e. Or else, it sounds like get or got. For example, **guante** as 'get,' **gesto** as 'her.'
[h]	Hache	The letter 'h' in Spanish is silent. For example, **hilo.**
[j]	Hotah	The letter 'j' sounds harsh or horse. But never as jump or jar. For example, **jirafa.**
[k]	Kah	The letter 'k' sounds similar as in the English language. It is pronounced as key or car. For example, **koala.**
[l]	Ele	The letter 'l' is uttered as like or lord. For example, **lobo.**
[ll]	double ele, elle	The double 'l' is spoken as the 'y' in yesterday. For example, **calle.**
[m]	Emeh	The letter 'm' is similar as in the English man or mother. For example, **modo.**
[n]	Eneh	The letter 'n' sounds similar as in the English note and no. For example, **nosotros.**
[ń]	enyeh	The 'ń' isn't another letter 'n'. This letter sounds as canyon, onion or lasagna. For example, **nińa.**
[p]	peh	The letter 'p' is similar to the sound in the English paste or pet. For example, **pelo.**
[q]	koo	The letter 'q' is spoken as curious. If it is written with 'ue' and 'ui' the letter 'u' is silent.

		For instance, '¿quién?' is spoken as *kien*. What's more, the '¿qué?' as *ke* (using the Spanish 'e'). For example, **qué, quién**.
[r]	ere	The letter 'r' sounds like brr at the start of a word. Or else, it sounds like brown or break. For example, **raton** as 'brr,' **crear** as 'break.'
[rr]	erre	The double 'r' sounds like 'r' at the start of a word. It is sound is much vibrated, as the sound of a vehicle accelerating. For example, **perro.**
[s]	ese	The letter 's' sounds similarly as in the English language sea or sorry. For example, **solo.**
[sh]	esse / hache	The 'sh' sounds as show or shampoo. For example, **show.**
[t]	teh	The 't' sound is pronounced as in English, even though the tongue needs to touch the back of your teeth like test and tea. For example, **tela.**
[v]	veh	The 'v' sounds are proncounced as the letter 'b.' However, your lips are touched slightly as voice or various. For example, **vecino.**
[w]	doble veh	The 'w' sounds have a similar pronunciation as in the English language wine and whiskey. For example, **kiwi.**
[x]	equis	The 'x' sound is spoken as 'gs' or 'ks' like in excited or explosion. For example, **xilófono**.
[y]	i griega / ye	The letter 'y' is the same as the double 'l.' However, it has a slight difference as yellow and crayon. For example, **yegua.**

| [z] | Setah | The letter 'z' is uttered as 'th' not as in zero or zip. For example, **zorro.** |

Are you now looking for ways to make it simpler for you to say these letters as a native Spanish speaker? Then there's no need for you to worry. You could look online for an audio file and listen to it to make sure you get it all right.

We suggest that you stay away from any translation software when learning how to pronounce any word in the Spanish language. The reason behind this is that such applications do not have the required accent to make you pronounce each word accurately. Make sure you look for real individuals speaking in the native Spanish language on different video platforms. These people tend to speak authentic Spanish, meaning you could learn more from them and much quicker.

E. Where to Go From Here

The best thing about this book is that you don't need to read them every chapter from the start to the end. Every chapter stands on its own, and it does not oblige you to finish any other of the chapters within the book. That setup saves you sufficient time if you have mastered particular topics but feel somewhat insecure about the others.

Therefore, make sure you leap right in. Now is a perfect time that you get your feet wet. If you not certain exactly where to start, you can look at the Table of Contents. Choose the topic, which appears to best suit your requirements and capabilities. If you are getting concerned that your existing background might not be strong enough, you could begin at the very start. From them, you could work way throughout the book.

Just bear in mind that learning the Spanish language is not a sort of competition. You must work at a pace, which fits your needs. Do not pause to read a chapter a second, third, or even fifth time many days later. Take note that you could adapt this book easily into your learning skills. You need to take note that you should have a positive and confident outlook towards this.

Indeed, you will make some mistakes. Everybody does – in fact; most native Spanish speakers always do. Your goal here is to speak and write. If you could make yourself understood, you have won the greatest part of the war.

F. The Stress Rules

You are already aware that Spanish words are stressed on the *last syllable* when they end in a consonant other than s or n. For example, **Gibraltar, Santander, El Escorial, Valladolild.** You see, they are stressed on the *syllable before last* when they end in s or n or a vowel. For example, **Valdepeñas, Toledo, Granada.**

When a particular word breaks either of such rules, an accent is written to highlight where the stress falls. For example, **civilización, José, Gifón, kilómetro, Cádiz, Málaga.** Every word ending in –ion bears that accent. Therefore, if you notice a written accent, you should stress the syllable where the accent is located. The only other usage of accents you must understand is that it is situated on *si* to distinguish **si** (yes) from **si** (if).

The only other usage of accents you must understand is that it is situated on *si* to distinguish **si** (yes) from **si** (if).

Vocabulary in Eating Out

Do you think you can eat your way to becoming fluent in Spanish? Well, maybe you can't, but the least you can do is learn about their culture in eating out, their food, and how they talk about it.

If you claim yourself as a certified food, you know that if there is a way to the heart of a culture and a person alike, it would be none other than food. Even your own hometown may have its prominent type of food, eating habits, food etiquette, and food culture that everyone loves and enjoys. These are all expressions of your place. The same thing applies to Spanish cuisine. Food plays a big role in Spanish culture, serving as an expression of friendship and love with others.

People love to talk about food, and it is among the universal topics of small talks most people are comfortable with. Thus, understanding Spanish food culture and vocabulary can go a long way. This is why there is no yummier way to learning Spanish than through Spanish cuisine. If you find it exciting, you are not alone. And while food is being discussed, you might want to know that *comida* is the Spanish term for food.

The Food Culture in Spain

Spain's food habits are known far and wide for its uniqueness. Drinking and eating are very important in Spanish culture, with bars found everywhere you look. There is always the excuse to socialize at a local drinking hole or grab some small-portioned appetizers, or what they call tapas. Many bars serve as hangouts and restaurants where Spaniards can watch futbol or soccer or football in the United States together.

However, the main difference in the food culture of Spain is when and how they eat.

Spanish Eating Habits and Manners

Spain's eating habits have primarily centered on work life. Spain runs on 11-hour workday a present although this is starting to change in some regions. Their workday begins at around 9 in the morning and finishes until 8 in the evening. For this reason, their mealtimes are significantly much farther apart compared to what other people are used to.

El Desayuno – Breakfast

Spaniards love to indulge in a light breakfast or *desayuno* in the morning before they head out to work. This is usually composed of coffee with milk or *café con leche* and a roll or pastry with jam, such as *bollos* or sweet rolls.

Due to the extremely long gap between their breakfast and *la comida*, that literally means the food but refers to lunch in this particular context, most people sometimes take a break in the middle of the morning to grab some snacks. The snack is often made up of *tapas*, such as the popular potato omelet or *tortilla de patata*.

La Comida – Lunch

Also known as *el almuerzo*, there is a strong belief among Spaniards that food must be completely enjoyed, making lunch a no-rush affair. When workers grab lunch around 2 in the afternoon, the workplace is normally shut down for 2 to 3 hours to give the employees a chance to go feast. Lunch in space is the day's biggest meal consists of three or even more courses. Drinking wine during lunch is also common, and this is usually a part of the price of the meal.

In Spanish culture, common foods for lunch include pasta or soup, a dish of fish or meat-filled with proteins, salad, and dessert-like *flan* or vanilla custard or just fruit. Wine, brandy, and coffee are common drinks enjoyed at lunch. You will almost always find lots of bread at all meals for wiping the plate clean.

Once the long lunch is over, it is common to take a short nap or *siesta*. There are even some parts of Spain where the law protects *siestas*. However, in larger cities such as Spain, it is no longer than common.

La Merienda – Snack

Due to the long workday, it is usual to stop to grab another snack around 5 or 6 in the afternoon. *La merienda* is similar to England's afternoon tea consists of small things like salami, bread, cheese, fruit, chocolate, and other types of small finger foods.

La Cena – Dinner or Supper

With 8 pm marking the end of the workday, Spaniards eat their dinner at around 9 or 10 in the evening. This is typically simple and small, unlike lunch, particularly because it is already so late. A common dinner meal is *arroz cubano*, which is composed of rice, tomato sauce, and a fried egg. Dinner still includes a small dessert of *flan*, cheese, or fruit and a salad.

Bocadillo de Medianoche - Midnight Snack

Average Spaniards go to bed around midnight daily, so it is common to hear about a *bocadillo de medianoche*. Churros are regularly picked up before going home after spending a night out and socializing at a bar. Some also enjoy a warm and nice cup of Spanish hot chocolate.

Sobremesa ("Over the Table")

In Spain, eating and dashing are rude. Sobremesa is a term used to describe the conversation's flow that takes place once the meal is finished. Spaniards don't just take time savoring their food but also the company of other people.

Traditional Spanish You Shouldn't Miss

What are the most common Spanish dishes? Standard diet in Spanish Mediterranean that features a lot of vegetables, fruits, healthy fats such as olive oil, and whole grains. Spain boasts of numerous flavorful and unique dishes, but the following traditional Spanish foods deserve to top your must-try list.

Paella

Paella is among the most traditional and common Spanish dishes. This is a saffron rice dish with meat and beans. There are lots of variations and veggies, shrimp, fish, and meat can also be used for toppings. The most traditional *paella* dishes use duck, rabbit, chicken, or even nails as primary protein even though the most common one is seafood *paella*. It doesn't matter where you find this because saffron rice is the one ingredient that remains unchanged. It is commonly eaten during lunch with the beautiful city of Valencia being its place of origin.

Tortilla Española

Probably the most often eaten and popular food in Spain is *tortilla Española,* a potato omelet found anywhere you go and pretty much everyone knows how to prepare it. While it sometimes contains other ingredients, the most traditional version is the omelet with just egg and potato.

Gazpacho

This is a tomato-based soup served chilled that can make you feel refreshed during summer days. It is very popular with most people eating it every single day. It also happens that traditional gazpacho is totally free from meat that makes it the ideal option for vegetarians. This is commonly made with ripe and bright red tomatoes, cucumbers, garlic, bread, olive oil, and peppers. This delicious food originates from Andalusia, the southernmost part of Spain where it can get really hot and as expected, boiling hot soup is not an option.

Patatas Bravas

With an English translation brave potatoes, *patatas bravas* is a staple on all *tapas* menus and the usual go-to option fans of vegetarian tapas. The potatoes are fried then served with spicy sauce. Spicy foods are not popular in Spain, yet this sauce is an exception to that rule. The sauce can vary from one region to another, but the potatoes remain the same.

Jamón Ibérico

No matter where you go, you can always see these ham legs being displayed everywhere. There are two types, namely black pigs (*jamón ibérico*) and white pigs (*jamón serrano*), with the former being more expensive. Meat is being thinly sliced from the leg and enjoyed with bread as *tapas* dish.

Albondigas

Also a staple on *tapas* menus, these Spanish meatballs are being served in rich tomato sauce. However, there are several variations. There are even some regions where they use squid for meatballs.

Chorizo

You have probably tried this in the past since it is now very popular all over the world. However, ask a Spain native, and they will surely tell you that Spain has the best *chorizos* you can ever find. It is a sweet and spicy sausage and often quite garlicky. This can be found in many other recipes to add richness and depth to the flavor.

Pisto

If France has *ratatouille*, Spain has *pisto*, an excellent vegetarian dish you can find around the country. This is made with aubergine, onions, tomatoes, bell peppers, and courgette. There are also times when this is topped with a fried egg.

Pollo al Ajillo

This one is classic comfort food for Spaniards. Pallo al ajillo is a garlic chicken dish cooked with thyme, rosemary, and a splash of sherry or white wine to create a comforting and rich flavor.

Chicharrón

This is the complete extravaganza of pork rind. It is a seasoned and fried pig skin dish that serves as a well-loved snack all over Latin America and different parts of Spanish.

Ceviche

It is a lemony seafood soup often served throughout the coasts of South and Central America. Every country has a unique style and flavor.

Dulce de tres leches

It is a super sweet and moist cake featuring three forms of milk, namely condensed, dried, and natural.

Churros

This is sugar-coated and crispy fried dough that no one can surely resist.

Patacone or Tostones

These fried and crisp plantain slices are a popular side dish all over Latin America.

Whether you are abroad or at home, try seeking out traditional dishes from the Spanish-speaking countries for you to better immerse in both the culture and language. Nothing beats the fun of indulging yourself while having an educational experience at the same time.

Must-Know Spanish Food Vocabulary

Does your stomach growl with the mention of food? As you have learned about the food culture and favorite meals of Spaniards, now is the time for you to start talking about them in Spanish.

Foods for Breakfast in Spanish

Breakfast is no doubt, the most vital meal of the day. Take note of the following words you can use when ordering your breakfast to fuel your day filled with adventure abroad.

- *Desayuno* - breakfast

- *Pan* - bread

- *Tocino* - bacon
- *Mermelada* – jam
- *Mantequilla* - butter
- *Bollos* - sweet rolls
- *Avena* - oatmeal
- *Pastelería* - pastry
- *Café* - coffee
- *Con* - with
- *sin* - without
- *Leche* - milk
- *Y* - and
- *Azúcar* - sugar
- *Yogur* - yoghurt:
- *Huevos* - eggs
- *Chorizo* – sausage
- *Huevo revuelto* – scrambled eggs
- *Tortilla* – omelet

Foods for Lunch and Dinner in Spanish

- *Plato fuerte* – entree

- *Comida* - food
- *Almuerzo* - lunch
- *Cena* - dinner
- *Arroz* - rice
- *Patatas* - potatoes
- *Sopa* - soup
- *Ensalada* - salad
- *Pastas* - pasta
- *Verduras* - vegetables
- *Pimiento* - bell peppers
- *Cebolla* - onions
- *Carne* - meat
- *Cerdo* - pork
- *Res* - beef
- *Pollo* - chicken
- *Calamares* - squid
- *Pescado* - fish
- *Camarones* - shrimp
- *Mariscos* - seafood

- *Aceite de Oliva* - olive oil
- *Tomate* - tomatoes
- *Pepinos* - cucumbers
- *Frijoles* - beans
- *Ajo* - garlic
- *Zanahoria* - carrots
- *Espárragos* - asparagus
- *Sal* - salt
- *Huevo Frito* - fried egg
- *Pimienta* - pepper
- *Vino* - wine
- *Bebidas* - drinks
- *Cerveza-* beer
- *Agua-* water
- *Cola* - soda
- *Té* - tea

Dessert Foods and Snacks in Spanish

- *Postre-* dessert
- *Bocadillo* - snack

- *Chocolate a la Taza* - hot chocolate
- *Queso* - cheese
- *Flan* - vanilla custard
- *Frutas* - fruit
- *Pera* - pear
- *Manzana* - apple
- *Guindas* or *Cerezas* - cherries
- *Fresas* - strawberries
- *Naranja* - orange
- *Sandía* - watermelon
- *Limón*- lemon
- *Nueces* - nuts
- *Higos* - figs
- *Bollito* or *Galleta* - cookie
- *Tarta* – cake
- *Ensalada de frutas* – fruit salad
- *Gelatina* – gelatin or Jell-O
- *Helado* - ice cream

Drinks – *Bebidos*

Upon arriving at a restaurant, the waiter will ask you if you would like a drink. Improving your refreshment vocabulary will let you get straight to browsing the restaurant menu:

- *Vino tinto* - red wine
- *Vino blanco* - white wine
- *Limonad* - lemonade
- *Té helado* - iced tea
- *Batido* - smoothie or milkshake
- *Jugo* - juice

Some common flavors of smoothie or juice you might want to order include:

- *Melón* - melon
- *Sandía* - watermelon
- *Frutilla or fresa* - strawberry
- *Uva* - grape

Seafood – *Mariscos*

- *Cangrejo* - crab
- *Langosta* - lobster
- *Atún* - tuna

Meats – *Carne*

- *Jamón* - ham
- *Lomo de cerdo* - pork tenderloin

- *Pavo* - turkey
- *Bistec* - steak
- *Codorniz* - quail

Vegetables and Fruits – *Verduras y Frutas*
- *Aguacate* - avocado
- *Acelga* - chard
- *Calabaza* - pumpkin
- *Berenjena* - eggplant
- *Espinaca* - spinach

Spanish Words Used in the Kitchen
- *Mesa* - table
- *Cocina* - kitchen
- *Horno* - oven
- *Microonda* - microwave oven
- *Estufa* - stove
- *Plato* - plate
- *Cuchillo* - knife
- *Servilleta* - napkin
- *Chucara* - spoon
- *Tenedor* - fork

- *Copa* - glass (for wine)
- *Vaso* - glass (for water)
- *Tazón* or *Cuenco* - bowl
- *Sartén* - frying pan
- *Olla* - pot
- *Cucharón* - ladle
- *Espátula* - spatula
- *Cubiertos* - cutlery

Verbs for Eating and Cooking in Spanish

- *Cocinar* - cook
- *Preparar* - prepare
- *Picar* - chop
- *Cortar* - cut
- *Pelar* - peel
- *Freir* - fry
- *Hervir* - boil
- *Saltear* - sauté
- *Hornear* - bake
- *Revolver* - stir

- *Batir* - whisk
- *Vertir* - pour
- *Medir* - measure
- *Cucharadita* - teaspoon
- *Cucharada* - tablespoon
- *Taza* - cup
- *Beber* - drink
- *Comer* - eat
- *Pedir* – order

Food Preparation
- *Filete* - fillet
- *A la plancha* - grilled
- *Asado* - roasted
- *Al ajillo* - in garlic sauce
- *Apanado or empanizado or empanado or *very regional word* - breaded
- *A la parrilla* - barbecued

Spanish Words and Phrases to Use When Ordering Food in a Restaurant

- *Restaurante* - restaurant
- *Camarera, Camarero* – waitress, waiter

- *Quisiera ___, por favor* - I would like , please

- *¿Me pone/trae _, por favor?* - Could I have _, please

- Tengo alergia a _____ - I'm allergic to....

- El menú - the menu

- No como _____ - I don't eat...

- La cuenta - the bill

- Tarjeta de Crédito - credit card

- Efectivo - cash

- ¿Qué me recomiendas? - What do you recommend?

- No me gusta eso - I don't like it.

- Está riquísimo - It's delicious.

Words and Phrases You Should Know When Dining in a Restaurant

Who can say no to eating? What is more important for you? Your happiness or your waistline? You will never regret it if you explore all the delicious and sumptuous local foods every time you go overseas. Spending some time at Spanish restaurants can play a big role in your Spanish language learning experience and cultural immersion.

Unfortunately, when traveling, it may be a bit difficult if not completely impossible to have access to a fully-equipped kitchen, not to mention that you may prefer to allot your time for exploring the sights instead of going grocery shopping.

Before you set foot on your destination, you can arm yourself with the following phrases and words that will help you order your meal like a true native Spanish speaker.

Finding Your Table

If you picked a swanky bistro often crowded with devoted patrons, it might be a good idea to make your reservation in advance. You can reach them through the phone then greet the other person on the line with a friendly salutation. The conversation can go like this.

"*Quisiera hacer una reserva para # persona(s).*" (I would like to make a reservation for # people.)

"*¿Bajo el nombre de quién?*" (Under whose name?)

On the other hand, if you are not the type who plans ahead and time, you can just go to a full restaurant by asking for a seat at the bar.

¿Podría sentarme en el bar? (May I sit at the bar?)

It is common in Latin America to be a bit suspicious when it comes to special dietary preferences. It is important to specify it with your server and inform them of the things you cannot eat. For example:

No como X. (I don't eat X.)

*Soy vegetariano, vegetariana (*I am vegetarian.)

Tengo alérgia a X (I am allergic to X.)

Make sure you double-check that all your orders don't contain things you can't or don't want to eat.

Navigating the Restaurant

- *restaurante* - restaurant

- *pedir* - to order

- *quisiera* - I would like

- *el menú* - the menu

- *camarero, camarera* - waiter, waitress

- *mesero, mesera* - waiter, waitress (Latin America only)
- *mesa* - table
- *plato* - plate
- *tenedor* - fork
- *cuchara* - spoon
- *cuchillo* - knife
- *servilleta* - napkin
- *cuenta* - bill
- *Tráigame la cuenta, por favor.* - Bring me the check, please.

The hand gesture of signing paper can translate smoothly enough. Many small restaurants in Latin America don't accept *tarjetas de crédito* or credit cards, so it is best that you carry some cash or *efectivo* with you in case of emergency.

Understanding Regional Food Traditions

Every time you travel, don't hesitate to ask questions to locals. You can always ask the waiter or waitress what he or she can suggest or recommend.

¿Qué me recomienda? (What do you recommend?)

¿Cuál es la comida típica de esta región? (What is the typical food of this region?)

More Useful Spanish Phrases for Dining

After you have brushed up on your knowledge about the Spanish counterparts of common English food and menu items, it is time for you to learn additional common phrases in Spanish that can come in handy during your conversation with your waiter or waitress or other people at the table.

Check out the following common Spanish phrases your waiter might use when taking your order:

- *¿Estan listos para ordenar?* (Are you ready to order?)

- *¿Qué desea beber?* (What would you like to drink?)

- *¿Qué desea comer?* (What would you like to eat?)

- *¿Qué quiere?* (What do you want?)

- *¿Lo siento/Lamento, no tenemos _____* (Sorry, we don't have____)

You can try to use these helpful Spanish phrases to answer the above questions:

- *Estoy/Estamos listos para ordenar.* (I/We are ready to order.)

- *Un momento por favor.* (One moment please.)

- *Quisiera _____.* (I would like ___.)

Use the following Spanish words when you ask questions to your waiter or waitress:

- *¿Qué nos recomienda?* (What do you recommend?)

- *¿Cuál es el plato del dia?* (What is the dish of the day?)

- *¿Cuál trae el plato?* (What is in the dish?)

- *¿Señor/Señora, la cuenta, por favor?* (Mr./Ms. the bill, please?)

- *¿Soy alérigico a ___* (I'm allergic to___)

These Spanish phrases can be used when talking to the people you are dining with:
- *¿Qué nos recomienda?* (What do you recommend?)
- *¿Qué te gusta hacer?/¿Qué le gusta hacer?* (What do you like to do?)
- *¿Como es tu comida?* (How is your food?)
- *¿Qué libro acabas de leer ?/¿Qué libro acaba de leer?* (What book did you just finish reading?)

Tips for Proper Spanish Etiquette for Dining

Do have plans to embark on a big trip to a Spanish-speaking country? There is a chance that you will eat at different delicious restaurants during your stay. Prior to embarking on your getaway, aside from learning the useful Spanish words and phrases, it is also important to arm yourself with some etiquette tips. For all you know, the same rules for etiquette that you follow in your country might not be applicable in the country you will travel to because of cultural differences.

Remember these tips for eating out:
- Don't forget to use eating utensils. You will be provided with a spoon, a knife, and a fork that you can use as you eat. Large spoons are meant for foods like beans and soup, while smaller ones are for desserts.
- Let the host eat first. Never dive into your food if your host hasn't eaten yet. Wait until your host starts eating or says, "¡*Provecho*!" or "¡*Buen Provecho*!" (Enjoy your meal) as this signals that you can also start eating your meal.

- Never dip your bread in your Spain. Dipping bread in the soup is regarded as rude in Spain. The truth is that it is not common to dip bread in pretty much anything, with sauces included.

- Make sure your hands stay visible. You have to put your hands on any side of your plate if you are not eating. It is considered suspicious if your hands are hidden. See to it that your elbows are also kept off the table while your hands stay visible.

- Engage in conversations because Spaniards love to do so! Don't be shy to talk about your family, your hobbies, or your day. Also, never be afraid to ask the people at the table some questions about themselves.

- Call over your waiter for your bill. It is seen as rude for waiters to bring bills to the table unsolicited. If you like to get your bill, try to catch the eye of the waiter and make that hand gesture as if you are writing something in mid-air.

Remembering these helpful and useful etiquette tips and practicing the useful Spanish words and phrases will ensure that you are well prepared every time you go out to eat at Spanish restaurants.
Do you feel confident with your Spanish vocabulary for eating out? Well, it means that you are now on your way to becoming a fluent foodie in Spanish! Discovering the culture through food is one of the best ways to understand how the locals socialize. Nothing beats the comfort of being able to share your experiences over a warm and delicious meal.

Asking for Directions

Knowing how to receive and give directions in Spanish is possibly among the most helpful things you can add to your skillset every time you travel around. Just imagine yourself getting disoriented in the middle of a strange new city, completely clueless about how you can get back to your hotel. This kind of experience can be quite disconcerting, but as long as you know how to ask directions from a local, then, it will be easy to avert such a stressful situation.

While getting lost in a strange city is one of the best ways to discover hidden gems, it is still imperative that you know how you can find your accommodation. Through memorizing directions in Spanish, you wouldn't have a hard time calling on them any time you need to.

If you ever find yourself lost amidst a Spanish-speaking country and you have no idea where the main square is or how you can get to your hotel, it is important that you know how to ask for directions or *pedir indicaciones*.

For instance, if you want to the main square or *plaza mayor* of the city you are visiting, you can ask *¿Me podría decir dónde está la plaza mayor?* (Could you tell me where the main square is?)

But this is just one example of how you can ask for directions. In this chapter, you will learn some words and phrases you can use for asking directions together with some tips on forming your own questions and a few handy vocabulary lists to help you understand the other person's response.

Don't be Afraid to Ask

It is important to remember that there is no such thing as a single right way of asking for directions in Spanish. While trying to form your question, you need to take note of several key verbs pertaining to the place or direction. For example, if you want to ask where something is, you need to use the verb *estar*. On the other hand, if you want to ask how you can get someplace, the verb *llegar* should be used. Lastly, if you don't have any idea about your current location and you want to identify where you are on a map, you need to use the verb *ubicarse.*

Take a look at the following examples of how to use the said verbs for forming your questions:

¿Cómo llego a la calle principal? (How do I get to the main road?)
¿Me podría decir dónde está la estación de buses? (Could you tell me where the bus station is?)
¿Nos podrías ayudar a ubicarnos en el mapa? (Could you help us locate where we are on the map?)

Pedir direcciones is another way of asking for directions in Spanish and is used interchangeably with *pedir indicaciones*.

Using Addresses

You might want to know that the structure of the street addresses often differs from one country to another. You can try to consult with a tourist guide prior to your travel for you to be more familiar with the local practices in the place you are visiting.

Most of the time, it is easier to understand addresses than what it might initially seem. For instance, among the most famous museums located in Bogotá, Colombia, is el Museo del Oro(Gold Museum) at Cra. 6 #15-88. At first, this may sound and looks like a complete jumble of different characters. However, Cra. 6 means that the museum is on Carerra 6, which you may refer to in English as 6th Avenue. The 15 is the name of the street (Calle 15), while the 88 refers to the distance from the intersection of the avenue and the street.

The sad news for travelers is that addressing conventions that are easy to understand are not used and followed everywhere, and there are even some streets that are left unnamed. For instance, in Costa Rica, you may encounter addresses like "200 metros al oeste de la escuela Fernández," that indicates a location 200 meters west of Fernandez school.

Know Your Directions

Since you now know the basics of how you can ask for directions, the next step is for you to understand these directions for you to follow them to your specific direction. Check out this list of the keywords you need to memorize so you can follow the directions given to you.

- izquierda - left
- derecha - right
- derecho, recto - straight ahead
- norte - north
- sur - south
- oeste - west
- este – east
- a la derecha - to the right
- a la izquierda - to the left
- al comienzo del/de - at the beginning of
- al final del/de - at the end of
- hacia el oeste - to the west
- hacia al norte - to the north
- hacia al sur - to the south

- hacia el este - to the east
- doblar, girar - to turn
- enfrente de - across from
- detrás de - behind
- al lado de - next to
- ¿dónde está...? - where is...?
- delante del/ de - in front of

Greetings

Of course, it would be impolite to just ask for directions without any greetings first. Here is a refresher of basic Spanish greetings you can use:

- hola - hello
- buenas - hello (at any time of days)
- ¿qué tal? - how are you doing?
- buenos días - good morning
- buenas noches good evening (night)
- buenas tardes - good afternoon
- hasta luego - see you later
- adios - goodbye

Roads

- dirección - address
- la calle - street

- carretera - highway
- bulevar - boulevard
- la avenida - avenue
- la carretera - main road
- cuadra - block (of a street)
- la intersección - intersection
- calle secundaria - sidestreet
- el callejón - alley
- a la vuelta - round the corner
- la rotunda - roundabout
- el callejón sin salida - cul-de-sac, dead end
- la esquina – corner
- manzana (Spain) or cuadra (Latin America) or – city block

Places
- el pueblo - village
- el Puerto – harbor
- el país - country
- los países - countries
- barrio - neighborhood
- plaza - square

- semáforo - streetlight
- el puente - the bridge
- la plaza de toros - bullring
- la galería (de arte) - art gallery
- las tiendas - shops
- el centro commercial - shopping mall
- el parquet - park
- el Mercado - market
- el casco antiguo - historic centre
- la frontera - border

Means of Transport
- a pie - on foot
- el autobus - bus
- en coche - by car
- el autocar - coach
- la moto - motorbike
- el avión – plane
- el barco - boat

Orientation and Directions
- coger - to take
- seguir - to carry on

- andar, caminar - to walk
- cruzar, atravesar - to cross
- todo recto - straight on
- lejos - far (away)
- cerca - near(by)
- bajar - go down
- subir - go up
- tirar para - head towards
- abajo - down(wards)
- arriba - up(wards)
- enfrente de - opposite
- detrás de - behind

Other Things to Say
- la pregunta - question
- pasear - to walk around, stroll
- dar una vuelta, dar un paseoto - go for a walk/stroll
- deambular - to wander aimlessly
- perdido - lost
- un paseo - stroll
- corer - to run

- kilómetro - kilometer

- mile – milla

- metro – meter

- la excusa - excuse

- estamos perdidos - we are lost

- está a un paseo - it's a stroll away

- ¿voy bien por aquí para ... ? - am I going the right way for ... ?

- está a una buena caminata - it's quite a way

- este parte de la ciudad me recuerda a Slough - this part of the city reminds me of Slough

More Spanish Speaking Terms to Use During Travels

- Escríbalo, por favor. (Write it down, please.)

- Hágame el favor de hablar más despacio. (Speak more slowly, please.)

- No entiendo bien el español. (I don't understand Spanish well. —)

- ¿Hay alguien que hable inglés? (Is there anyone who speaks English?)

If you wish to know where something is, you just need to ask "Excuse me, where is the _____?" by saying, "Disculpa, donde esta el/la _____?" Pay close attention to the reply, and you will be good to go. You can also verify what you heard using hand movements.

Here are some sample questions and sentences on how you can use the vocabulary words above for forming some directions.

- Hasta donde topa. (Until the end of the street.)

- *Bajas por ahí.* (Go down that way.)

- *Gira a la izquierda/derecha.* (Turn left/right.)

- *Das vuelta a la izquierda/derecha.* (Turn left/right.)

- *En contra esquina de....* (Kitty-corner from...)

- *En la esquina.* (On the corner.)

- *A espaldas del/de la ...* (Behind the ...)

- *¿Cómo llego al/ a la ... ?* (How do I get to the ... ?)

- *Rodea el/la ...* (Go around the ...)

- *¿Qué tan lejos queda el/la ... del/de la ... ?* (How far is the ... from the ... ?)

- *¿Hay un/una ... cerca de aquí?* (Is there a ... around here?)

- *¿Dónde puedo tomar un taxi?* (Where can I take a taxi?)

- *¿Sabes si está por aquí?* (Do you know if it's around here?)

- *Creo que estoy perdido/a.* (I think I'm lost.)

- *¿Pasa por aquí el camión que va a ... ?* (Does the bus to ... pass by here?)

- *¿Dónde está...? ¿Dónde están...?* (Where is...? Where are...?)

- *¿Está lejos? ¿Está por aquí?* (Is it far away? Is it near here?)

- *¿Por dónde se va a...?* or *¿Cómo puedo llegar a...?* (How do you go to...?)

- *¿Dónde estamos aquí en el mapa?* (Where are we on the map?)

- *Busco...* (I'm looking for...)

- *Estoy perdido (perdida* if you are female). (I'm lost.)

- *El bar está en frente de la catedral, a sólo cinco cuadras de la plaza mayor.* (The bar is across from the cathedral, just five blocks from the main square.)

- *Gira a la izquierda y camina por el callejón hasta que llegues a la Avenida de Las Américas.* (Turn left and walk through the alley until you come out at Avenue of the Americas.)

- *Sigue recto tres cuadras y luego dobla a la derecha.* (Continue straight for three blocks and then turn right.)

- *Avanza tres cuadras.* (Go ahead three blocks.)

- *Sigue derecho dos cuadras.* (Go straight ahead two blocks.)

- *Subes todo derecho.* (In Mexico, many people use the phrase to say "Go straight ahead" every time they talk about a direction where the land's topography is higher.)

- Spain: *¿Dónde puedo coger un taxi (un autobús)?*/ Latin America: *¿Dónde puedo tomar un taxi (un autobús)?* (Where can I catch a taxi (a bus)?)

Take note that there are others used for bus depending on the region include *bus, camión, colectivo, camioneta, guagua, góndola, micro, Pullman,* and *microbús*, You have to be careful when you use the verb *coger* in some areas of Latin America since this may have an obscene meaning.

Additional Directions and Sample Conversations

If you ever find yourself exploring the streets of San Juan, Quito, or Cartagena, you may notice that street signs are found on the buildings' sides instead of sticking out the ground around the intersections. You may even discover that these street signs show abbreviated forms of carretera, bulevar, or calle.

In Latin America, there are several street signs that include dates. This is because most cities in Latin America use significant dates from the history of their country as names of prominent streets. So, don't panic if the person giving you direction instructs you to turn right on *9 de Julio*.

Sample Conversation #1:

Clara: *Disculpe, señora. Estoy totalmente perdida. ¿Me podría ayudar a ubicarme en este mapa?* (Excuse me, ma'am. I'm completely lost. Could you help me figure out where I am on this map?)

Woman: *Estamos aquí, cariño, Al lado del estadio de fútbol.* (We are right here, dear. Next to the soccer stadium.)

Clara: *¡Ah, claro que sí! Necesito reunir con mis amigos en una hora para cenar. ¿Usted conoce el restaurante Buena Vista en el centro histórico? ¿Cómo llego allí?* (Ah, of course! I need to meet up with my friends for dinner in an hour. Do you know the Buena Vista restaurant in the historic city center? How do I get there?)

Woman: *Es muy fácil. Sigue esta calle cinco cuadras al sur hasta que llegues a la plaza mayor. De allí, gira a la derecha en la calle*

10 de agosto y camina solo una cuadra. Allí lo verás enfrente de la estación de buses. (It's very easy. Follow this street five blocks south until you reach the main square. Then turn right onto August 8th street and walk just one block. You will see it there in front of the bus station.)
Clara: *¡Muchísimas gracias, señora!* (Thank you so much, ma'am!)

Sample Conversation #2:
Tourist: *Disculpe, ¿podría decirme dónde está la plaza de toros?* (Excuse me, could you tell me where the bullring is?)
Antonio: *Siga recto y coja la segunda calle a la derecha.* (Carry straight on and take the second street on the right.)
Tourist: *¿Está cerca de la catedral?* (Is it near the cathedral?)
Antonio: *No, para ir hasta allí tiene que cruzar todo el centro.* (No, to get there you'll have to go right across the centre.)
Tourist: *¿Hay algún autobús que pase por allí?* (Is there a bus that goes nearby?)
Antonio: *Sí, al doblar esta esquina tiene la parada del veintitrés, que le deja al lado.* (Yes, when you turn this corner you'll see the stop for number 23, which leaves you next to it.

Sample Conversation #3:
Katrina: *¿Cómo puedo ir al centro de la ciudad?* (How do I get to the city center?)
Juancho: *Cruce la calle, gire a la derecha, cruce de nuevo, gire a la izquierda y ya estará allí.* (Cross the street, turn on the right, cross again, turn on the left, and you'll be there.)
Katrina: *¡Gracias!* (Thank you!)

Sample Conversation #4:

Rosa: ¿*Cómo puedo ir a este barrio*? (How do I get to this neighnorhood?)

Fernando: *Siga todo recto, gire a la izquerda, cruce la calle y ya estará allí.* (Go straight, turn on the left, cross the street and you´ll be there.)

Rosa: *¡Gracias!* (Thank you!)

Even though the GPS on your smartphone can be a handy resource, you will never know when you will be left with a dead battery or with no signal at all. This is why it is a must that you know how you can ask for directions in Spanish way before you embark on your trip to a Spanish-speaking country.

Two Tips for Conversation When Asking for Directions

1. Be specific. Always stick with key terms for the places you want to go to during your conversations with other people. You might need the directions to a shopping mall (*el centro comercial*), the grocery market (*el mercadoII*) or general shops (*las tiendas*). While these three can all be summed up as shops, keep in mind that they differ in terms of the specific type of shop. If you wish to explore different tourist attracts, you have to detail if you want to see art historic center (*el casco antiguo*), an art gallery (*la galería de arte*), or a park (*el parque*),

2. Always be friendly. Locals are always delighted when tourists show courtesy and ask for their help with a smile. Don't forget to include some basic greetings together with the phrases you learned. You will surely score bonus points if you also use the local variations like *buen dia* that is used in several countries instead of the more common and popular *buenos dias*.

Traveling by Bus & Train

Traveling in Spain as well as other countries and destinations that speak Spanish can become so much easier when you are familiar with several Spanish words and phrases. Knowing how to book tickets, ask for directions, and find out the times of trains and busses can make a big difference in your travel experience. This vocabulary can come in handy if you have plans to take a quick city break, go on an extended holiday with the family, or travel or business.

Traveling in Spain

As far as travel is concerned, Spain visitors can choose from three primary options, assuming that hiring a car is out of the equation. The primary forms of getting around the city are by train or bus. Another option is traveling by air as the country is dotted by lots of national and local airports alike. Although English is spoken and understood at the majority of larger airports and train or bus stations, this is not really the case at the local or smaller airports or stations. However, it doesn't need to be a problem since you only need a few words for you to arrange your journeys and book your tickets without any hassle.

In most countries, public transportation is a need, and for those who have plans to visit or travel to a Spanish-speaking country, there is always a high chance that you will need to use one form of public transportation or another. This makes it very helpful to study some of the key and common vocabulary words, phrases, and expressions.

Cultural Facts about Transportation in Spanish-Speaking Countries and Destinations

- Due to rapid growths in population and sometimes, lack of properly planned infrastructures, most towns and cities face some serious problems with transportation. Since public transportation is often insufficient or inefficient for covering transportation needs, most of the time, the streets are crowded with too many vehicles that lead to pollution and traffic jams.

- *Carro* or car is also referred to as *coche* or *auto*.

- Bus is called guagua in Spain and Cuba and camión in Mexico.

- Transmilenio is the enormous public transportation system being used in Bogotá, Colombia.

Means of Transportation in Spain

Among the most common forms of public transportation in the majority of Spanish-speaking countries are taxis and buses. Both are often found in small and big cities but more often than not, buses transport commuters from one town to the next while taxis transport their passengers only within the limit of the city. Below is a list of Spain's common transportation vehicles:

- (el) bus, autobus - bus

- (la) buseta - small bus

- bus escolar - school bus

- (el) tren   /trehn/ - train

- (el) carro - car

- (el) colectivo - shared taxi

- (el) taxi   - taxi, cab

- (el) camion - truck

- (el) avión - plane
- (la) camioneta - van, pickup truck
- (la) avioneta - light aircraft
- (el) helicopter - helicopter
- (el) bote - small boat
- velero - sailboat
- (el) barco - ship
- (el) yate - yacht
- (la) canoa - canoe
- (la) motocicleta - motorcycle
- (la) bicicleta - bicycle
- (el) metro - subway
- (el) autocar - coach
- ambulancia - ambulance
- cohete – rocket

Important Basic Transportation Vocabulary and Phrases in Spanish

Travel is among the biggest reasons why people learn and master new languages. It can be quite hard to get around somewhere if you don't speak the language of the place you are going to. So, if you have plans to visit a Spanish-speaking country, you need to pay close attention to the words and phrases being used, especially in public transportation. After all, this might be your first concern the moment you arrive at your destination so you can get to the place where you want or need to go, whether it is to your hotel or anywhere else. Here is some basic vocabulary to learn to do this:

- departures – salidas
- arrivals – llegadas
- passport – el pasaporte
- money – el dinero
- suitcase – la maleta
- insurance - los seguros
- bag – el bolso

Useful Expressions and Actions

The following herbs will help you in moving around any Spanish-speaking country:

- viajar en bus - to travel by bus
- subir al bus - to get on the bus
- coger el bus - to catch the bus
- bajar del bus - to get off the bus
- pedir un taxi - ask for a cab
- ir a pie - to go on foot
- llegar - to arrive
- irse - to go

- salir - to leave, to depart
- abordar - to board
- desembarcar - to disembark
- embarcarse - to embark
- manejar, conducer - to drive (a car, a truck)
- montar - to ride (a bike, a motorcycle)
- pilotear - to fly (a plane)
- poner gasoline - to put gas

Below are some other useful expressions that may come in handy during your visit to a Spanish-speaking country:
- (la) tarjeta de viaje - travel card
- (el) pasaje de ida - one-way ticket
- (el) pasaje de ida y vuelta - round-trip ticket
- (la) estación - station
- (la) parada de bus - bus stop
- (el) trancón - traffic jam
- (la) ruta - route
- (el) viaje - trip
- el conductor - driver
- el transbordo - transfer
- pagar el boleto - pay for the ticket

Useful Transportation Phrases

- *¿Hablas Inglés?* (Do you speak English? -)

- *¿Cómo puedo ir a...?* (How can I get to...?)

- *Un boleto, por favor.* (One ticket, please.)

- *¿A qué hora sale el próximo autobús/tren para (Barcelona)?* (At what time does the next bus/train to (Barcelona) leave?)

- *¿De dónde sale el autobús/tren para (Madrid)?* (Where does the bus/train to (Madrid) leave from?)

- *¿Este autobús para en (Córdoba)?* (Does this bus stop in (Córdoba)?)

- *Me bajo en la próxima parada.* (I get off at the next stop.)

Important Public Transportation Phrases in Spanish

- estación de metro - metro station

- estación de ferrocarril - railway station

- taquillas de billetes - ticket office

- ventanilla - ticket window

- máquinas de billetes - ticket machines

- ventanilla de infomación - information window

- sala de espera - waiting room

- llegadas - arrivals

- salidas - departures
- vía - track
- andén - platform
- plano del metro - map of the metro
- línea de metro - metro line
- mapas de carreteras - train route map
- parada - stop
- horario - schedule / timetable

Traveling by Train in Spanish-Speaking Countries

When you buy train tickets, you have to ensure that you specify if you need a round-trip or a one-way ticket, the specific class you want to sit in and if there is a discount or a reduced rate.

- billete / boleto - ticket
- un billete / boleto de ida y vuelta - round-trip ticket
- un billete / boleto de ida solamente - one-way ticket
- la primera clase - first class
- segunda clase - second class
- tarifa reducida - reduced rate
- descuentos para estudiantes/ niños - discount for students/children
- tarifa normal - standard rate
- abonos - season tickets

- el horario - timetable
- precios - price
- el destino - destination
- el viaje – journey

Some questions you can ask when buying train tickets include:
- *¿Cuánto es un billete?* (How much is a ticket?)
- *Quisiera un billete de ida y vuelta.* (I would like a round trip ticket.)
- *Quisiera un billete de ida.* (I would like a one-way ticket.)
- *¿Va usted a...?* (Do you go to...?)
- *¿Dónde puedo comprar un billete?* (Where can I buy a ticket?)

Types of Train Tickets

Traveling by train in Spain is a cost-effective and quick way to discover and explore the country. There are three types of tickets available on the high speed AVE train, namely:
- preferente - business
- turista - tourist
- club - first

Prices may also vary according to your chosen time:
- llano - standard
- punta - peak

- valle -off-peak

Types of Trains

Depending on whether or not you are in a hurry, you can choose from any of the following types of trains common in Spanish-speaking countries:

- interurbano - regional express
- cercanías - commuter train or local train
- exprés - quick nighttime train
- rápido - quick daytime train
- estrellas - night trains

Once you are on the train, there are several areas that you might want to check out:

- portaequipaje - luggage rack
- coche comedor - dining car
- coches camas - sleeper or sleeping cars
- coche fumador - smoking car

Train Transportation Questions

If you are taking the train, don't forget to know the arrival and departure time. You also need to check the horario schedule, or better yet, you can also ask some questions to the station assistant.

- *¿A qué hora sale el tren?* (What time does the train leave?)
- *¿Cuándo sale el tren para ...?* (What time does the train for...leave?)

- *¿Cuándo llega el tren de ...?* (When does the train from...arrive?)
- *¿Cuánto tiempo dura el viaje?* (How long does the journey take?)
- *¿A qué hora llegará allí?* (When does it arrive there?)
- *¿Cuál es la próxima parada?* (What is the next stop?)
- *¿Cuántas paradas más hasta ...?* (How many more stops until...?)

It is also important to always be careful.
- *Por favor, no asomarse por la ventana.* (Do not lean out of the windows, please.)

Traveling by Bus in Spanish-Speaking Countries

It doesn't matter if you are a tourist who travels across the country on a luxury bus, an expat who wants to catch the local bus across town, or a backpacker who rides on one of the popular chicken buses, there are several key phrases you can use to catch the bus to make your Spanish trip easier, more fun, and more convenient.

- *¿Me puede avisar cuándo lleguemos a (...)?* (Can you tell me when we get to (...)?
- *¿Me puede decir donde me bajo del aútobus?* (Can you tell me where to get off the bus?)
- *¿Podría decirme cuando me tengo que bajar?* (Could you tell me when I have to get off?)
- *¿Ya pasó el autobús?* (Did the bus already come by?)

- *¿Me bajo aquí?* (Do I get off here?)

- *¿Tengo que cambiar de autobús?* (Do I have to change buses?)

- *¿Tengo que bajarme aquí?* (Do I have to get off here?)

- *¿Pasan autobuses los fines de semana?* (Do the buses run on weekends?)

- *¿Pasa el autobús en el fin de semana?* (Does the bus run on the weekend?)

- *¿Este autobús va al centro?* (Does this bus go downtown?)

- *¿Este autobús va a (...)?* (Does this bus go to (...)?)

- *¿Se para este autobús en (...)?* (Does this bus stop in (...)?)

- *¿Hasta qué hora pasa el autobús en la noche?* (How late does the bus run at night?)

- *¿Cuánto tarda en pasar el bus?* (How long before the bus comes?)

- *¿Cuánto cuesta el pasaje en autobús a (...)?* (How much is the bus fare to (...)?)

- *¿Cuánto es el pasaje de autobús?* (How much is the bus fare?)

- *¿Con qué frecuencia pasan los autobuses?* (How often do the buses run?)

- *Quiero bajarme en la próxima parade.* (I'd like to get off at the next stop.)

- *¿És este el autobús a (...)?* (Is this the bus to (...)?)

- *¿A qué hora tengo que tomar el aútobus?* (What time do I have to catch the bus?)

- *¿A qué hora sale el último autobús?* (What time does the last bus leave?)

- *¿Cuál es la próxima parada?* (What's the next stop?)

- *¿Cuándo llega el próximo autobús?* (When does the next bus arrive?)

- *¿Cuándo pasa el próximo autobús?* (When does the next bus come by?)

- *¿Cuándo sale el próximo autobús a (...)?* (When is the next bus to (...)?)

- *¿Dónde tomo el autobús a (...)? / ¿Dónde tomo el autobús a (...)?* (Where do I catch the bus to go to (...)?)

- *¿De dónde sale el autobús?* (Where does the bus leave from?)

- *¿Dónde está la estación de autobuses?* (Where is the bus station?)

- *¿Dónde está la parada del autobús?* (Where is the bus stop?)

- *¿Dónde está la parada para ir a (...)?* (Where is the bus stop to go to (...)?)

- *¿A qué hora es el próximo autobús a (...)?* (What time is the next bus to (...)?)

- *¿Está ocupado este asiento?* (Is this seat taken?)

- *¿Cuánto dura el viaje?* (How long is the trip?)

- *¿Dónde puedo comprar un boleto?* (Where can I buy a ticket?)

Tips for Travelling by Bus, Train, and Other Public Transportations in Spain

Traveling in Spain is somewhat straightforward. The most part of preparation can be easily done from the comforts of your home before you go on your trip. For example, tickets can be bought from a travel agent or even online before you travel.

Most of the large Spanish cities and towns have their own websites complete with information about traveling around and to the area. It usually includes specific details about local trains and buses. Some bigger stations also have automatic ticket machines from which you can buy your tickets using your credit card that will let you travel to other stations around Spain.

Below are a few tips that can help you during your travel in Spain:

- Even though the names of most Spanish cities are just the same in Spanish and English, it is not unanimously the case. Make sure that you use the Spanish names for certain cities like Seville or Sevilla in Spanish.

- If you don't feel too confident about asking for and buying tickets and asking for other details in Spanish, a helpful tip is to write down your request or question. This is especially useful when time is short or in busy situations. This can also reduce the possibility that misunderstandings will occur.

- It is also useful to carry around some small maps. Every time you ask for directions, it will be easier for you to demonstrate on your map and you will also find it easier compared to listening to the directions spoken in a language you are not familiar with.

- Write down or print out important travel phrases and always have this with the rest of your travel documents. It can serve as your quick reference guide.

To get the best out of this vocabulary, it might also be better if you can review Spanish numbers and brush up on telling the time in Spanish.

Take note that transportation can differ from country to country, and as a result, some vocabulary might change as well. The bus is the perfect example here. Even though most Spanish speakers will understand autobus, locals might also use other names to refer to this means of transportation, such as guaga in some countries in Central America, colectivo in Argentina, and camion in Mexico. Study the vocabulary in this chapter but don't forget to talk to locals for you to know the characteristic language customs and quirks of the Spanish-speaking destination you are visiting.

Introducing & Talking about Yourself

Knowing how to start a conversation is one of the very first things you have to know for you to learn to speak Spanish. How will you even practice if you don't know how to strike a conversation in the first place? And of course, the best way to start any conversation is to introduce yourself.

Getting Started: Basic Vocabulary and Phrases Introduce Yourself in Spanish

Take a look at some of the basics of how you can introduce yourself to the Spanish speaking world:

- ¡Hola!

Wouldn't the world be boring if hello is the only word you can use to say hello to others? There are a lot of options to choose from if you want to greet other people. You can say hi, good evening, good afternoon, good morning, what's up, hey, and so much more. When it comes to Spanish, you can also choose from more options aside from *hola*.

1. *Buenos días.* (Good morning.)

2. *Buenas tardes.* (Good afternoon/evening.)

3. *¿Qué hay?* (What's up?) (loosely translated)(This is a very informal version you can use only with family, friends, etc.)

4. *¿Qué tal?* (How's it going?) (A bit more informal)

5. *Buenas.* (Hello.) (This is something you will hear often on the streets or every time you walk into shops and others.)

- Yo me llamo...

After you say hello to someone, the next logical step is for you to tell them what your name is. There is no way that you can start a conversation with someone when you don't know that person's name or when that person doesn't know who you are. Again, you got several options here:

1. *Mi nombre es.* (This is a very practical option that means "My name is...")

2. *(Yo) me llamo...* (This is most commonly used with the literal translation "I call myself".)

3. *Soy*...* (If you are a big fan of brevity, you will love this version that similar to saying "I'm...")

Getting Deeper

Even though it is a must that you know the other person's name for you to start a conversation with him or her, if this is all you have to say, you can expect that the chat is going to be a very short-lived on. What are the other things you can say about yourself, then?

- *Soy de... Vivo en...*

As mentioned earlier, *soy* is a verb that means "I am..." It is very helpful to remember that if you will follow it with the preposition *de*. This will then mean, "I am from..."
For example, *Soy de Chicago* means I am from Chicago.
But, just because you are from somewhere might not mean that you also live there. It would be wise to share this little piece of

information about yourself to someone else. You can say *vivo en* that means I live in.

For example, Soy de Chicago pero vivo en Madrid means I am from Chicago, but I live in Madrid.

- *Soy...*

You see this verb again, and that is no surprise since this is quite important. One more thing you might want to mention about yourself is what you do or what your job is.

Soy un(a) estudiante/ profesor(a)/ dentista/ abogado(a). (I am a student/ teacher/ dentist/ lawyer/,)

Take note that there is no change in gender here.

- *Tengo X años.*

There is a bit of a difference when you say your age. Surprisingly, there is no need to use estar or ser for this one. You need to pay close attention since this is one thing that most English speakers often find themselves in trouble. You are not 20 years old in Spanish, and instead, you have 20 years.

Tengo 20 años. (I have 20 years.) This means that you are 20 years old.

- *Me gusta...*

Me gusta is also a useful expression you have to know when you want to introduce or talk about yourself. Many English speakers might find this expression a bit tricky since its construction is somewhat different from how it is said in the English language. Its literal translation is "To me it is pleasing..."

To make it less complicated, you can just stick with using the construction with several verbs in the infinitive. You can say, "To me it is pleasing to do (insert verb here)."

Me gusta leer/ jugar al baloncesto/ ir al cin / cocinar/. (I like to read/ play basketball/ go to the movies / cook/.)

Step-by-Step Method to Introduce Yourself in Spanish

After learning some of the basic words and phrases used for introducing yourself in Spanish, below are steps you should follow to talk about yourself.

1. Hello, It's nice to meet you.

Nice to meet you and hello are two phrases in Spanish that you must know. As stated earlier, any introduction will possibly start with any or both of these phrases.

Hola, es un placer conocerte. (Hello, it's nice to meet you.)

2. My name is _____.

It is a simple phrase that means "my name is," and you only need to add the phrase "Mi nombre es." You can then say your name after it.

Mi nombre es _____. (My name is _____.)

3. I am from _____.

Where do you come from? Are you from Asia? Africa? Europe? America? Just add your country's name to the phrase. In this example, Mexico is used.

Soy de México. (I'm from Mexico.)

4. I live in _____.

Where do you live right now? Add the name of your country or city if it is famous for the phrase. Mexico City will be used as an example because Mexico was used in the sample above.

Yo vivo en la Ciudad de México. (I live in Mexico City.)

5. I am _____ years old.

As stated earlier, the way you say your age in Spanish is different. You have to make yourself familiar with Spanish numbers for this, and these are not really difficult.

Tengo 27 años de edad. (I'm 27 years old.)

6. I am _____.

How about your position? Are you a yoga teacher? A teacher? A potato industry lawyer? Potato salesman? This is a very important question people love to ask. You just need to use *soy,* which means *I'm*, then add your specific position.

Soy maestro. (I'm a teacher.)

7. I've been learning Spanish for _____.

For how long have you been trying to learn? Have you been learning it for a year or for a month?

He estado aprendiendo español por un año. (I've been learning Spanish for a year.)

8. I'm learning Spanish at _____.

Do you learn Spanish at home or at school? It is a good line you should know and use every time you introduce yourself.

Estoy aprendiendo español en Spanish101.com. (I'm learning Spanish at Spanish101.com.)

9. One of my hobbies is _____.

This is now the time for you to move onto your hobbies or personal hobbies. You will surely need a line about your hobbies when you introduce yourself in Spanish.

Uno de mis pasatiempos es leer. (One of my hobbies is reading.)

10. I enjoy listening to music.

You can use another line to talk about your hobbies. You could use something else.

Me gusta escuchar música. (I enjoy listening to music.)

Now, you have learned the top 10 basic lines for introducing yourself in Spanish. There are still a lot more you will learn later on, but this is a simple and easy start that newbies can put to good use. After all, starting easy is what matters.

Other Methods to Introduce Yourself in Spanish

Even if you just know a little Spanish, you will find it easy to introduce yourself to a Spanish-speaking person. There are several methods of how you can go about it.

Method #1 to Introduce Yourself

Just follow these tips, and you will be well on your way to connect with someone even when the other person doesn't necessarily speak your own language.

1. To say hello or hi, just say say "Hola" or "OH-la." This rhymes with "Lola" and note how Spanish has a silent letter h.

2. To introduce yourself, you can just say "Me llamo" then follow this with your name. For example, *"Hola, me llamo Rita"* means "Hi, I'm Rita."

3. To formally ask for the name of the other person, ask someone's name in a formal way, say "¿Cómo se llama usted?" This means, "What is your name?"

4. When talking to a child or in an informal setting, say "¿Cómo te llamas?" This also means, "What is your name?"

5. If the person responds, you can say "Mucho gusto." This phrase means "much pleasure" or "pleased to meet you" less literally.

Method #2 to Introduce Yourself

The second method might be a bit less common method of self introduction, but this is easier to learn and is also perfectly acceptable.

Majority of the steps here are just the same with the ones in the first method but in the second step wherein you are introducing yourself, you can"Hola" followed by "soy" then your name. You pronounce soy just as how you do in English. "Hola, soy Rita" means "Hello, I'm Rita."

Method #3 to Introduce Yourself

This third method is also not as common in most areas, unlike the first one, but it is probably the most straightforward way for people whose first language is English.

You can use "Mi nombre es" on the second step and followed by your name. This means that if your name is Rita, you may say: "Hola, mi nombre es Rita."

No matter what specific method you choose to use, never be afraid to sound a bit silly. You will be understood if you follow these directions. This is not to mention that even the feeblest attempts of speaking Spanish will be highly honored and appreciated in almost all Spanish-speaking areas.

Vocabulary and Grammar behind These Introductions

There is no need for you to understand the exact meanings of what you are saying or what the grammatical relationships of the words are to each other when it comes to introducing yourself. However, if you are curious or if you have plans to seriously learn Spanish, you might be interested to know more about it.

Just like how you probably guessed it, hello and hola are essentially the same word. People who are familiar with etymology or the study of origins of words think that this word dates back to the 14th century at least before Spanish and English alike came to existence in their present form. Even though it is not clear how the term came about in Spanish, there is a chance that its origin can be traced back in the German language as a means of trying to get the attention of another person.

In method #1 above, *me* means "myself." It is obvious to see that it has an etymological relationship with "me" in English. *Llamo*, on the other hand, is a form of *llamar*, a verb, and this actually means "to call." So, when you say "*Me llamo Rita*," this is the direct equivalent of "I call myself Rita." Llamar is being used in many similar ways as "to call," like when calling a person over the phone or calling out to someone. In English and Spanish alike, verbs, where the person refers to doing something to herself or himself, are called reflexive verbs.

The main reason as to why there are two methods used with llamar to ask for a person's name is because Spanish sets some differences between informal and formal, or also known as familiar and formal ways of addressing people. This was also done in English before, with thee, thine, and thou being informal terms at a certain period. However, in contemporary English, your and you can be used in informal and formal situations alike. Despite the regional variations as to how Spanish distinguishes between these two forms, it will be safer for foreigners to use the formal form with adults and those who have authority figures.

Soy is one of the forms of *ser*, a verb, and this means "to be." In the last method, *mi nombre es* is the word-for-word equivalent of "my name is." Similar to soy, *es* also comes from *ser*.

Introduce Yourself

Take a look at how you can introduce yourself in Spanish with the following common introductory questions as well as how you could answer them:

Como te llamas? / Cuál es tu nombre? (What's your name?)
Mi nombre es.../Me llamo... (My name is...)
De dónde es usted? (Where are you from?)
Soy de... (I'm from...)
Cuantos años tienes? (How old are you?)
Tengo... años. (I'm... years old.)
Cuál es tu trabajo? (What's your job?)
Soy un/una... (I'm a/an...)
Tienes hermanos/hijos? (Do you have any siblings/children?)
Tengo... hermanos/hijos. (I have... siblings/children.)

No tengo... hermanos/hijos. (I don't have any siblings/children.)
Qué te gusta hacer? (What do you like to do?)
Me gusta... (I like...)

Sample Conversations for Self Introduction

Now that you have learned the basics, it is time for you to put everything together. Here is a couple of sample from people who are introducing themselves. Both of them are native English speakers who study or live in English. These examples are going to use the phrases mentioned above together with some additional information about themselves.

Sample Conversation #1:

Hola, me llamo Nick y soy de los Estados Unidos. Vivo en España y soy profesor de inglés. Tengo veintiséis años. Tengo una mujer que se llama Ana y un perro pequeño cuyo nombre es Joey. Llevo 8 años estudiando español, y tengo un masters en la lingüística española. Me gusta estudiar español porque siempre me han gustado las lenguas y las palabras y poder hablar con otro grupo de gente es algo que puede ser muy gratificante y beneficioso.

English Translation: Hello, my name is Nick, and I'm from the United States. I live in Spain and am an English teacher. I'm 26 years old. I have a wife named Ana and a little dog whose name is Joey. I have been studying Spanish for 8 years, and I have a Masters in Spanish Linguistics. I like studying Spanish because I have always like languages and words, and being able to speak with another group of people is something that can be very rewarding and beneficial.

Sample Conversation #2:

¡Buenos días! Soy Ana. Tengo veintisiete años. Soy de Chicago, pero ahora vivo en una ciudad de España que se llama Zamora. Soy profesora de inglés en un instituto. Al volver a los Estados Unidos, voy a seguir con mis estudios.

Me gustaría hacer un doctorado en la literatura española. Pero, por ahora, estoy contenta de vivir en España y ir mejorando mi español y aprendiendo más de este país tan maravilloso. En mi tiempo libre me gusta leer, ver la tele, y pasar tiempo con mis amigos, mi marido y mi perro.

Estudio español porque la historia del país me fascina. No es solo eso, sino también la cultura me encanta y la gente es muy amable.

English Translation: Good morning! I'm Ana. I'm 27 years old. I'm from Chicago, but now I live in a Spanish city called Zamora. I'm an English teacher in a high school. Upon returning to the United States, I'm going to continue my studies.

I would like to get a doctorate in Spanish literature. But for now, I'm happy living in Spain and improving my Spanish and learning more about this wonderful country. In my free time, I like to read, watch TV, and spend time with my friends, my husband, and my dog.

I study Spanish because the history of the country fascinates me. It's not only this, but also I love the culture, and the people are lovely.

Introducing yourself is no doubt a very crucial aspect of taking your initial steps into learning and speaking the Spanish language. If you wish your language to get to a higher level, you have to practice how to speak it. And if you couldn't even tell someone who you are, how will you expect to engage in conversations with them?

The words, phrases, and tips mentioned above are only some of the many ways to let people know more about who you are. Since you now have a good base to get started, you can go out there and start looking for someone who can talk to. Try to practice as much as possible, and you will be well on your way to becoming a better Spanish speaker in no time at all!

Useful Phrases When Shopping

Hand-sewn scarves made from alpaca hair, fresh ceviche, a cold cerveza, refreshing coconut water or *agua de coco* and tapas. No matter what you want and crave for, the Spanish-speaking world got you covered.

Unfortunately, money won't buy you everything you need and want. You also need the right phrases and words for you to find the best shops and get the most reasonable prices.

How disappointing it would be to spend your whole afternoon looking for handmade alpaca sheets only to end up with machine-made polyester blend instead. This kind of disaster can happen even to the most seasoned travelers.

Unless you learn and master how to go shopping like the locals and bargaining with the shopkeepers, you will always stay as a complete gringo or foreigner. Aside from that, how else will you get the perfect souvenirs to bring back home with you? The last thing you want is to be the traveler who only brings back some corny souvenir shirts.

Shop Like a Boss in Spanish – Why Is It Important?

Every time you travel to any Spanish-speaking country, it is only expected that you go shopping. That's just how things work. You will need some basic supplies like foods, toiletries, and maybe even a few medicines. You also need souvenirs and more this and that. This is the point when you wouldn't want to go on a shopping spree like an obvious foreigner or *extranjero* because your goal is to shop like a pro.

Below are some of the top reasons why you should know a few important shopping vocabularies in Spanish:

- Markets are great. Why will you bother to go abroad if you won't explore the sights, tastes, smells, and sounds of the local markets?

- You will stay oriented. Equipping yourself with this vocabulary can help you locate things. You could ask for recommendations from locals as to where you can purchase some quality items for lower prices. It will also prevent you from getting lost during your trip.

- Keep yourself safe from getting ripped off. When you are at the market, you can score better deals when you can affirm your knowledge and don't stammer or stutter over prices and vocabulary. If you sound like the foreigner as you are, people will assume you have no idea what you are doing, and they might just charge you even more.

- Always stay on your feet. As expected, markets are also among the top and most common places where foreigners can get robbed. A pickpocket can literally rob you or shopkeepers may overcharge you for products. When you speak confidently, and you sound like you really know what you are doing, you can lower the chances that you will experience such misfortunes.

- The culture of Latin America includes bargaining. It doesn't mean that people will try to take advantage of you or be cruel to you. They just want to get the best prices possible, and they do it even with their fellow countrymen. Don't expect that there won't be a small debate before your money can leave your hands. It is natural and normal, and people don't find it offensive if you try to lowball them. It is merely one aspect of buying something. Just make sure you don't try to bargain at more formal establishments such as department stores and supermarkets. Do this only with individual salespeople and at smaller marketplaces.

- Try to sound cool like locals, and do it casually. The vocabulary you will find here is important to help you become more fluent in Spanish. You can break this out as you chat with friends and recount your adventures as you shop for souvenirs in the market.

- Bargaining is also a form of skill. After you practice with Spanish street vendors, you will soon discover that you also got better as you negotiate with English-speaking vendors in other areas. Also, bargaining in Spanish is a great speaking practice. You will be able to think on your feet a sound more fluent.

Essential Spanish Words and Phrases to become a Savvy Shopper

Ir de Compras (Going Shopping)
- entrada - entrance
- salida - exit —
- horario de atención - business hours
- abierto - open
- cerrado - closed

You might see a notice that says "cerrado al mediodía" and this means closed at noon. It doesn't mean that they will be closed exactly at noon and instead, the idea here is that the shop will be closed during lunch hour.

- (Latin America/Spain), jale (Latin America), tire - pull

- empuje – push

Such signage will ensure that you won't look like a fool as you angrily force the doors in the exact wrong direction.

- feriado – holiday/long weekend

Las Tiendas (The Shops)
Do you need or want to know where you can buy things? If yes, you should know how to ask for the right and exact type of store.

- tienda - shop/store

- local - storefront

- tiendita - little shop (selling a plethora of little things)

- grandes almacenes - large shopping depot, storehouse

- boutique - boutique

- mercado - market

- supermercado - supermarket

- ferretería - hardware store

- centro de compras - shopping center

- mercado o feria artesanal - artesanal market (this is where you go for souvenirs or recuerdos that were handcrafted (hechos a mano).)

- centro comercial - mall

- agencia de viajes - travel agency
- carnicería - butcher
- cafeteria - café, snack bar, buffet
- licorería - liquor store
- pastelería - bakery (desserts)
- panadería - bakery (bread)
- pescadería - fish stand
- farmacia - pharmacy
- peluquería - hair salon
- florería - flower shop
- joyería - jewelry store
- gasolinera - gas station (remember this word during your trip in latin america since this usually a great place to make change for your large bills, atms, and go for the bathroom.)
- juguetería - toy store
- librería - book store (this falsely sounds like "library," but a library is called biblioteca.)
- tienda de ropa - clothing store
- papelería - paper/office supply store
- tienda de deportes - sports store
- zapatería - shore store

- tienda de música - music store

¿Dónde comprar? (Where to Buy?)

It is not enough that you just know what you need or want to buy since you should also know where it is. Below are some sample questions you can ask:

    ¿Conoce un lugar donde venden _____? (Do you know where they sell _____?)

    ¿Conoce un lugar donde realizan _____? (Do you know a place where they make/do/perform_____?)

If you need the expert opinion of a local to help you make a decision, you can start a conversation with someone and ask:

    ¿Conoce algún_____ por aquí cerca? (Do you know of a _____ around here?)

You could also try to be more specific to explain the types of qualifies you to expect the place to have. You can use a question like:

    ¿Dónde queda la tienda de ropa más (cercana/chévere/económica/?) (Where is the (closest/coolest/cheapest) clothing store?)

You just need to insert one more type of store apart from *tienda de ropa,* and you can ask about pretty much anything.

If faced with some good choices, but you are unsure which is a better option, you can ask, *"¿Cuál me recomienda?"* (Which one do you recommend to me?)

Cositas (Little Things)

When you go shopping, you want to say all sorts of things. Whether you need restaurant and food vocabulary, soccer equipment, textile, and artisanal items, here are some words you might encounter and hear at street markets.

- artesano(a) - craftsman

- artesanías - artisanal goods

- mamacitas - affectionate term for women manufacturers of artisanal goods

- cooperativa - cooperative (It is a great term to hear in artisanal markets, since goods crafted, distributed, then sold by a cooperativa benefit a community group. These community cooperatives are required to have a Fair Trade certification.

- proyecto comunitario - community project (Crafting artisanal goods is usually acommunity endeavor so you might want to ask about the person or people behind the product you are buying. As much as possible, try to support local endeavors.

- Comercio Justo - Fair Trade

- organic - organic

- de la selva / jungle - from the jungle

- De la montaña / del monte (bosque) - from the mountains / from the forest

- de la playa / del mar - from the beach / from the sea

- todo natural - ,

- casero/a - homemade

- hecho/a a mano - handmade

- tallado/a - carved

- tejido/a - knitted

- cosido/a - sewn

- porcelana - porcelain

- cerámico/a - ceramic

- fibras - fibers

- uña, garra - claw

- diente de (tiburón, tigre, tigrillo) - (shark's, tiger's, large cat's) tooth

- concha - seashell

- tinte - dye

- semilla - seed

Textiles (Textiles)

Prior to discussing prices of textiles, you have to identify what you are buying in the first place. "¿Qué tipo de tela es?" (What type of fabric is this?) or "¿Qué material es?" (What material is this?). Don't forget to double-check tags.

- tela - fabric

- cuero - leather

- algodón - cotton

- franela - flannel

- lana - wool

- terciopelo - velvet

- licra - lycra

- de oveja - from sheep

- de alpaca - from alpaca

Cómo Pedir (How to Ask)

Is it necessary to be super polite? After all, the saleslady you were talking to was really nice. Spanish learners might find it a bit challenging to ask for things. When talking to older people, you might want to stay on the safe side and stick with polite grammar and phrases in the third person. The following polite phrases can be used when interacting with vendors.

Muchas gracias, señor(a). (Thank you very much, sir/ma'am.)

Quisiera uno de esos, por favor. (I would like one of those, please.)

If you are talking to an elderly woman, you can use doña to show a higher level of respect. For more casual encounters, you are generally free to stick with less formal language. Less formal language is actually encountered if you want to sound more local. Below are a few common informal phrases you can use for shopping situations:

Dame uno, por favor. (Give me one, please.)

¿Me pasas eso, por favor? (Can you pass me that, please?)

There are several ways for you to explain your likes and dislikes to people. This can help them understand the items you are interested in and those that you aren't.

Este(a) no me gusta tanto. (I don't like this one so much.)

Quiero este(a)/Quiero ese(a). (I want this/that.)

Me gustan aquellos(as) de allá. (I like those over there.)

¡Me encanta este(a)! (I really like / love this one!)

Don't expect that you will always get exactly what you want. There are times when stores might run out of things you are looking for. If you are out of luck, you might hear these things?

Ya no tenemos. (We don't have that anymore.)

Se acabó. (We ran out of that.)

Calidad (Quality)

Your goal when you want to buy anything anywhere is to look for "Los Tres B's" or The Three B's, namely bueno, bonito y barato or good, nice, and cheap. Save this in your mind and make this your new mantra every time you visit the Mercado.

Below are several words you need to know when talking about the quality of items.

- bonito - pretty

- elegante - elegant

- barato - cheap

- economic - affordable

- feo - ugly

- lujoso - luxury

- hermoso - beautiful

If you trust the shopkeeper enough to help you choose the right items for you, you want to ensure that they know you are paying attention.

Deme los más bonitos/jugositos/maduros/, por favor. (Give me the prettiest/ juiciest/ripest ones please.)

If you end up with a lower quality or damaged item, such as one broken egg out of a dozen, return this to the vendor then say *"Cámbieme este, por favor"* (Change this one for me, please).

Tamaños y Tallas (Sizes)

Did you figure out the difference between a talla and a tamaño? Both of them mean size but you are referring to different kind s of objects here. This one is rather a sneaker. Talla is basically used for shoes and clothes while tamaño is applicable for other items.

¿Qué talla de pantalón lleva usted? (What pants size do you wear?)

¿Cuál es la talla de su camisa? (What's your shirt size?)

¿Qué número/talla de zapatos lleva usted? (What shoe size do you wear?)

As far as sizes are concerned, make sure you translate sizes into European sizes before going shopping, or you might have to go through a few trials and errors to determine what fits. You might still need to try on several items anyway since shoes and sizes are cut different in a bit in various corners of the globe. Shoes are usually narrower and smaller in Latin America, while pants are often cut for much shorter legs.

- talla (pequeña/mediana/grande) - small/medium/large size

- no me queda (bien) - it doesn't fit me / suit me well.

- me queda bien - it fits me / suits me well.

- me queda muy grande - it's too big on me.

- apretado/a - tight

- suelto/a - loose

- me aprieta aquí - it's too tight here.

- ¿Puedo probármelo/a? - Can I try it on?

Hablar del precio (Talking About Prices)

¿Cuánto cuesta/vale? (How much is this?)

¿Cuál es el precio más bajo que me puedes dar? (What's the lowest price you can give me?)

¿A cuánto está? (How much are you asking for this?)

There are times when it can turn into a fiasco when actually buying products in small markets and shops. Unless the store is well-equipped for high volumes of tourists or shoppers, there is a big chance that no one will have any change. After you agreed on a certain price and you are ready to, ask the vendor,"*¿Me puede cambiar un billete de 20?*" (Can you give me change for a 20?). If the shopkeeper replies with a frustrated head shake or a sigh, you know you will have to embark on a journey to get some change. The person who makes the sale is often in charge of looking for a change from their nearby acquaintances and friends. They will walk around and ask *"Présteme monedas"* (Loan me some change!) or *"¿Tiene cambio/suelto?"* (Do you have any change?)

How to Bargain Smartly

This is now the time when you will have to know how you can bargain properly to get the best deals possible. This is what you have always wanted to learn, anyway. Instead of memorizing nice phrases for negotiation, there are phrases only true marketplace insiders know. These are the phrases you would want to invest on your own, or you can hear these from locals as they try to be persuasive after a long time of innocently overpaying for items or getting ripped off.

Your goal is to sound like an actual local when you go shopping. You would like to take vendors by surprise and watch their eyes gleam with respect or even amusement. There are phrases you can use to show you actually know what you are doing and you mean serious business.

For starters, there is something good shopkeepers will happily do for you, and that is, to offer you package deal to buy more things. Whether you are on your own shopping for several items or you are with your friends, try to make as many purchases as you can happen in just one place. If possible, avoid scattering your purchases across various vendors.

Look for a shopkeeper who sells most of the things you need to purchase and ask the vendor, "¿Me puede hacer un descuento si compro_____?" Insert all the products you wish to buy in the blank space. Try to sound casual as if you suddenly thought of buying two more items to save more cash. Once the shopkeeper answers with the expected "sí," this is the time to name your price. For example, you and two of your friends each want to purchase a beautiful alpaca scarf from a certain cart. The vendor already informed you that the price is $10 apiece. That's pretty expensive, right? Well, you can still get a good deal from this. Look at the vendor shrewdly and say "Dame 3 por 20" with confidence. Say it as a statement and not as a question. Don't sound unsure, apologetic, or soft. You will still pay well at around $7 per piece. You are not robbing the vendor. It is fair enough, and he will surely agree to the price instantly. This is better for you, yet he knows that someone else may even try for something lower.

On your next trip, you were on your own, and you want to purchase a pretty handcrafted necklace. You passed by one vendor offering a necklace for $14 while the one you are talking to now is asking for a price almost twice than that, $22. Will you just take this price? No, you will handle it as if you are a local.

Say *"La señora de allá me lo dejó en $12."* (The lady over there would give it to me for $12) or *"Pero allá cuesta $12"* (Over there it costs $12). This will let the vendor know that you are comparing prices and asking around. You are aware of the prices. The vendor may even say things such as how his necklace is a better one. Or can also get a new price that is in the ballpark. Let's say the vendor tells you *"Okay, te lo dejo en $15."*

You can try the following phrases to convince him to give it to you for the lowest price possible:

¿Cuál es el precio final final? (What's your final final price?) – It may sound a bit risky, but it may also work.

Bah, ¡déjamelo en $12 y me lo llevo! (Leave me at $12, and I'll take it now!)

¡Ya para llevármelo ahorita! Para no volver... (Alright already, let me walk away with this now! So I don't have to come back...) It pretty much says that both of you know that you are just playing a game, so they better give you a good price to get it over and done with.

¿Cómo arreglamos? (How do we fix this?) It will make the vendor see you as a nice guy who just wants to find a good solution. Both of you know that some prices are much better, but you choose to purchase from the vendor.

¿Cuánto es lo último para llevármelo ahorita? (What's the lowest price if I buy it on the spot?)

Aahh, porfaaa. (Awww, please...) There are two options you can try if you want to say this phrase. You can look tired of the price bickering, and you are on the verge of walking away, or you can also put on your big sad puppy eyes.

Tome, tome (C'mon, take my money already.)
Shopping for decorations and souvenirs is a different concern since these are non-essentials. On the other hand, what if you want to shop for some delicious tropical fruits? You heard about how locals pay cheaper, and you have also seen the prices. Or maybe you have spent some time in the town and you are fed up with people who still don't offer good prices for your day to day items. Below are some go-to phrases you can use to handle such a situation.

Amigo, yo sé cómo son los precios. (Hey buddy, I know how the prices are.)

¡Vivo aquí y gano un sueldo ecuatoriano! (I live here and earn an Ecuadorian salary!) Just insert the specific country where you are bargaining in. If you don't want to spend more than one dollar for something, you will surely appreciate this phrase.

Pero la semana pasada usted me lo dejó en_____ (But last week, you gave me __[price]___.) There are times when prices of stuff in the markets fluctuate during a change of seasons of when there is poor crop. Never assume that people are just lying to you. With the use of this phrase, you are pretty much saying that you are familiar with the price and you even imply that the same person offered you the right price in the past and you are curious about what happened with the sudden price change. You can get a true answer, or you may also get a reasonably lowered price. Finally, make sure all your transactions end with "muy amable" (thanks / you're very kind) or "Muchas gracias," (thanks so much). With this knowledge, you will soon negotiate better and wiser with vendors!

Vocabulary for Conversing with a Pharmacist or Doctor

Whether you are traveling to Latin America or Spain on business or vacation, there are some simple medical phrases in Spanish that you will surely want to add to your current Spanish language survival kit.

It is never easy to be surrounded by a foreign language, especially when you need to navigate the local health care system or you ever find yourself face to face with a pharmacist or doctor and you have to explain your particular illness. Being equipped with some medical Spanish phrases can make the whole experience so much easier. With a bit of luck, you shouldn't find yourself in a situation where you will need to use these medical Spanish words and phrases. However, it is still a must that you make yourself familiar with these. You might be in a situation where you need to purchase a medicine from a pharmacy, and you have to explain where you feel the pain and what your particular problem is. Or maybe you just need to get a bandage, a few sleeping pills for your long haul flight, or a bottle of cough syrup.

- Tenemos una emergencia. - It's an emergency! / We have an emergency.

- ¡Es una emergencia! - It's an emergency!

Common Medical Spanish Phrases You Can Use and Hear at the Doctor's Office

- Tengo dolor. - I have pain.

- Tengo dolor de estómago. - I have a stomach ache

- Tengo dolor de cabeza. - I have a headache.

- Tengo dolor de garganta. - I have a sore throat.
- Tengo dolor de muelas. - I have a tooth ache.
- Tengo dolor de oídos. - I have sore ears.
- No me siento bien. - I'm feeling sick.
- Estoy enfermo. - I'm sick.
- Me siento débil. - I feel weak.
- Me siento mal. - I feel unwell.

Spanish Medical Phrases to Describe Where It Hurts

These phrases can come in handy if you want to describe where it hurts.

- Me duele el brazo. - My arm hurts.
- Me duele la cabeza. - My head hurts.
- Me duele la pierna. - My leg hurts.
- Me duele la rodilla. - My knee hurts.
- Me duelen los dedos. - My fingers hurt.
- Me duele el pie. - My foot hurts.
- Me duele el tobillo. - My ankle hurts.
- Me duele el hombro.- My shoulder hurts.
- Me duele el ojo. - My eye hurts.
- Me duele la muñeca. - My wrist hurts.

- Me duele la espalda. - My back hurts.

Spanish Medical Phrases Doctors Use When Asking about Symptoms

Once you visit a doctor, the professional will ask you about the symptoms you are feeling:

- ¿Tiene dolor? - Do you have pain?

- ¿Que tipo de síntomas tiene? - What kind of symptoms do you have?

- ¿Donde le duele? - Where does it hurt (you)?

- ¿Tiene fiebre? - Do you have fever?

<u>Illnesses</u>

These are some of the common conditions and illnesses in Spanish.

- la alergia - allergy

- la diabetes - diabetes

- el resfrío - cold

- la gripe - flu

- la artritis - arthritis

- la picadura de abeja/avispa - bee/wasp sting

- la insolación - sunstroke

- la herida - injury

- la fractura – fracture

People
- El doctor/La doctora/ La médica/ El médico/ - The **doctor**
- La enfermera/El enfermero - The nurse
- La cirujana/El cirujano - The surgeon
- La/El dentista - The dentist
- La oculista/El oculista - The eye doctor
- La paramédica/El paramédico/ - The paramedic
- La otorrinolaringóloga/El otorrinolaringólogo - The ear, nose and throat doctor

Spanish Medical Phrases to Use at the Pharmacy

Symptoms
- estoy enfermo - I'm ill
- me encuentro mal - I don't feel good
- me duele la cabeza - I've a headache
- me duele ... - my ... hurts
- el dolor - pain
- el escozor - stinging
- el sarpullido - rash
- la inflamación, la irritación - inflammation
- el picor - irritation

- el resfriado - cold
- estoy constipado - I'm bunged up (with a cold)
- estoy resfriado - I have a cold
- la tos - cough
- vomitar - to vomit
- toser - to cough
- desmayar - to faint
- la fiebre - fever
- la gripe - flu
- el esguince - sprain
- el corte - cut
- el calambre - cramp
- la rotura, la fractura – break, fracture
- me he roto ... - I've broken my ...
- me he cortado - I've cut myself

Anatomy
- el ojo - eye
- la cabeza - head
- el cuello - neck
- la espalda - back

- la garganta - throat
- la mano - hand
- el brazo - arm
- el dedo - finger, toe
- la pierna - leg
- el estómago - stomach
- el pulmón – lung
- la barriga – belly, tummy

Treatments
- la medicina - medicine
- el comprimido - tablet
- la pastilla - pill
- el jarabe - syrup
- la pomada – cream, ointment
- el antibiótico - antibiotic
- el antiinflamatorio - anti-inflammatory
- el antihistamínico - antihistamine
- el inhalador - inhaler
- el paracetamol - paracetamol
- el colirio - eyedrops

Other Things to Say
- el accidente - accident
- el hospital - hospital
- urgencias - accident and emergency
- la farmacia - chemist
- la ambulancia - ambulance
- la farmacia de guardia - out-of-hours pharmacy
- ¡pobrecito! - poor thing!
- ¿cómo te encuentras? - How do you feel?
- llama una ambulancia - call an ambulance
- tengo que ir al hospital - I need to go to the hospital

Sample Conversations
Sample Conversation #1:
Doctor: *Tengo entendido que le duele el estómago.* (I understand that your stomach has been hurting.)
Maria: *Sí.* (Yes.)
Doctor: *¿El dolor es constante, o viene y se va?* (Is the pain constant, or does it come and go?)
Maria: *Viene y se va.* (It comes and goes.)
Doctor: *¿Está libre de dolor a veces?* (Are there times when you are free of pain?)
Maria: *Sí.* (Yes.)

Doctor: *¿El dolor le viaja a otra parte del cuerpo?* (Does the pain travel to another part of your body?)
Maria: *No.* (No.)
Doctor: *¿Se pone peor cuando come?* (Does eating make it worse?)
Maria: *Sí.* (Yes.)
Doctor: *¿Eructa o expulsa gases?* (Are you burping or passing gas?)
Maria: *Sí, las dos cosas.* (Yes, both.)
Doctor: *Le voy a examinar el vientre.* (I'm going to examine your abdomen.)

Sample Conversation #2:

Rosa: *Buenas tardes. Creo que he comido algo en mal estado.* (Good afternoon. I think I've eaten something that was off.)
Pharmacist: *¿Cuáles son los síntomas?* (What are the symptoms?)
Rosa: *Tengo náuseas, dolor de estómago, y me ha salido un sarpullido.* (I've got nausea, a stomach ache and I've come out in a rash.)
Pharmacist: *Desde luego, parece una intoxicación alimentaria.* (It definitely sounds like food poisoning.)
Rosa: *¿Y tiene algún remedio?* (Have you got something for it?)
Pharmacist: *Tome estas pastillas, y si mañana no se encuentra mejor, vaya al médico.* (Take these tablets, and if you don't feel better tomorrow, go to the doctor.)

Learn to Deal with Business Situations and Discuss the Weather

Business and weather are two important things that you also need to learn if you wish to study the Spanish language. Spanish is no doubt, one of the most widely spoken languages all over the world. A big chunk of the population not just uses Spanish as their mother tongue as they also bring it with them if when they move to nations such as the United States, the United Kingdom, and elsewhere. With the popularity of Spanish, it is obvious that this is something that you should know. Spanish is also extremely useful when doing business as it can open up doors of opportunities for you that English-only speakers will never get to enjoy. If you have decided to take that leap and learn Spanish, there are several business-related phrases to help you get by whatever your situation or level is.

Spanish Phrases to Use in Business Situations

1. La reunión es a las... (The meeting is at...)

Reuniónes (meetings) play a big role in all business environments, and it is a key phrase you should know when your schedule is filled with meeting after meeting.

2. Necesito ayuda, por favor. (I need help, please.)

Although there are times when you have to endure it until you can, there will also come a time when it is an absolute necessity to ask for help. Be very polite about it by adding por favor at the end, and you will never regret your decision at all.

3. Estoy en ello. (I'm on it.)

Everyone knows how today the business world has become a cutthroat and fast-paced environment, so see to it that you also let your Spanish-speaking colleagues that you are on top of everything even if you are not.

4. Enviar un correo electrónico. (Send an e-mail.)

Most correspondence and communication both inside and outside the world of business takes place online. Although technically Enviar un correo electronic is the right way of saying Send an email. You can also get rid of the word electronic for you to sound more like a native speaker.

5. La sala de juntas. (The meeting room.)

It is almost impossible to work in an office without hearing la sala de juntas every now and then. Many of your reunions may even take place there.

6. Perder el tiempo. (Waste time.)

While it is always possible to waste time in meetings, you can try to reduce gossips so that people won't assume that you are intentionally wasting time in the first place.

7. Tiene experiencia en estas cosas. (He/she has experience with these things.)

It can come in handy if you know the specialties and skills of your colleagues. After all, if you ever need help in the future, it just makes sense to look for the most experienced person.

8. Estoy trabajando a tope. (I'm working full-out.)

It is a good phrase to have handy if you feel overwhelmed with all the work piling in front of you. This is the polite way of saying that you have enough already.

9. ¿Puede decirle al jefe que estoy enfermo y que no podré venir hoy? (Can you tell the boss I'm sick and can't come in today?)

Everyone needs personal or sick days, and you will need a great phrase to tell your boss if you feel a bit under the weather. You may even impress your Spanish-speaking employer if you inform them about it using their native language.

10. Me pongo en ello ahora. (I'll get to it right now.)

Do you a have an impending deadline that requires you to set aside everything else. This is the phrase that will let your colleagues know that task at hand is your priority. This can also be a way to get someone off back if they continue to ask you to do something else.

11. Contrato fijo/indefinido. (Permanent work contract.)

All jobs need a good amount of negotiation, and it is good if you know how you can get exactly what you want. Contrato fijo/indefinido is permanent and contrato temporal means you will be on board on tempoerary basis.

12. La comercialización es de alta prioridad. (Marketing is a top priority.)

It might be a bit odd to say this if you just have basic Spanish knowledge, but if you are at the conversational level, this phrase is perfect for the workplace. Using this will make you sound knowledgeable.

Spanish Weather Vocabulary

Talking about the weather is undoubtedly the most interesting conversation, the smallest of small talks, and the ultimate icebreaker no matter where you go.

The weather is one thing everyone knows about. It is also something everyone has an opinion on, making this a great topic for conversations if you are just getting started in learning Spanish. Do you want to be genial at the market? Does the silence in the elevator make you feel awkward? Why not discuss the weather? Spanish expressions related to water can be broadly broken down into three primary categories. These are times when the weather is, times when there is some kind of weather, and times when the weather does.

Times When the Weather "Is"

In these weather conditions, you have to use estar instead. You probably recall this as the verb that means to be, and this is used to discuss a non-permanent state. It fits here because the weather is definitely something not permanent in this world.

- Está despejado - It is clear

- Está nublado - It is cloudy

- Está soleado - It is sunny

- Está tormentoso - It is stormy

- Está lloviendo - It is raining

- Está ventoso - It is windy

- Está nevando - It is snowing

Times When the Weather "Does"

There are weather phrases where you will use hacer, a verb that means to make or to do. In this case, this is used for describing what the weather does.

- Hace frío - It is cold

- Hace calor - It is hot

- Hace fresco - It is cool

There are times when you can also sum up everything with these expressions:

- Hace mal tiempo - The weather is bad

- Hace buen tiempo - The weather is nice

Times When "There is" Some Weather

Finally, there are cases when you use verb form hay in order to imply that there is some sort of exciting weather.

- Hay niebla - It is foggy (literally "there is fog")

- Hay viento - It's windy (literally "there is wind")

Hay, hace, está? What is the rule here?

Hace is typically used for describing the weather's general feel like it is cold or warm or windy. Está and hay are more specific in general.

You can spend lots of time trying to understand and figure out certain situations, but it is just best that you remember every delicious piece of weather vocabulary as a phrase. This will keep you from getting stuck on whether you should use hay or hace.

Exciting Weather Expressions in Spanish

There are several pretty colorful English expressions about the weather, such as raining cats and dogs. The same also applies in Spanish.

Tuck up the following expressions up your sleeve when it is raining really hard:

- ¡Llueve a cántaros! - It's raining pitchers/buckets!

- ¡Llueve a mares! - It's raining oceans!

If all the rain gets you down or if someone you know is having some difficulties in life, this rain-phrase also means "this too will pass":

- Siempre que llovió, paró - Whenever it rained, it stopped.

These phrases are used when it is cold enough to freeze off everything:

- ¡Hace un frío que pela! - It's so cold it burns your skin!

- ¡Me estoy congelando! - I'm freezing!

When the weather becomes a bit warmer:
- ¡Ay, qué calor! - What heat!

- ¡Es un horno! - It's an oven!

Practice & Revision of Your Spanish Vocabulary

Spain is an amazing place, a country rich in history dotted with snow-capped mountains, sophisticated cities, vast monuments, and stone castles. And if you feel like you are now ready to explore the country yourself, you could now start practicing and revising your Spanish vocabulary before you pack your bags and go.

Everyone will surely remember and treasure those days as they walk through the lovely streets and greet the smiling faces of locals. Sadly, a lot of people often ruin these first impressions by going on their Spanish trip without even trying to improve or practice their Spanish vocabulary at all.

Once they set foot on the country, the experience is not as rich and pleasant as they expected it to be, and they might even encounter some translation problems. After a few years, these stories of cute and innocent mistakes may sound funny, and you might get a good laugh as you remember them.

But, if it is actually happening in the present, you may feel a horrible sense of shame about how you were so careless to the point that you will wish that you took the time and made an effort to actually practice Spanish.

Read on some helpful tips on how you can practice your grammar and speaking skills before you go on your Spain trip or any trip to other Spanish-speaking countries. These will help you avoid getting into embarrassing situations and just have a great and memorable time during your stay!

Start by Practicing and Honing Your Spanish Grammar

Can you say that you know and are familiar with Spanish grammar? Yes, pretty much everyone has heard about how Spanish is among the easiest to learn languages in the world, but it wouldn't hurt if you double-check all the rules you already know.

Most students who apply to Spanish schools such as universities and colleges just think that it will be easy to do their admission essay and that they don't need any grammar once they are done with it. They assume that others will understand them. Well, don't go down this wrong route of thinking. Practice your grammar and your Spanish as a whole because you will need this every single day.

Below are several ways on how you can practice your Spanish grammar to make the process easier:

- Consistent approach – Try to spend 10 to 15 minutes a day to master your Spanish grammar. You can start one to two months before you travel. This doesn't sound that scary, right? You just need 15 minutes every day, and you will become better once the day of your trip finally arrives. You can also use any type of educational material, including online resources and textbooks. You can also look for a teacher who can explain to you everything you will need.

- Books – Reading can also help you memorize and recall grammatical structures. Books give you an image or context related to grammatical patterns. It will help you get a better understand of what you want to learn while letting you remember the basic rules. Go for books originally written in Spanish since this can provide you a better grip in practicing Spanish grammar.

- Magazines, newspapers, and blogs – It is a specific type of reading. Some resources make use of specialized language. Media, on the other hand, is among the few sources that will let you practice the new language you will face abroad.

It will surely help you take your Spanish grammar to the next level.

Pay Attention to Your Pronunciation

There are several things you should and shouldn't do when practicing and revising your Spanish vocabulary. There are a few improper recommendations that can mislead people who want to learn Spanish productive and consistently.

Dos

- Podcasts, video blogs, radio, and others – Sources with chatting will be enough here, including sports or music radio with interview breaks, interesting programs, or beauty, lifestyle, and how-to video blogs. These courses often have conversations with the simple everyday language you will speak soon. You will be better off if you choose an entertaining source as this can help you practice Spanish as you actually speak it.

- Visit Spanish Speaking Clubs. Don't say no when the opportunity to practice Spanish comes knocking at your door. Speaking with native Spanish speakers in your country can also help. They can give you advice, or they can also correct you if you request them to do so. You can also ask them questions about their country.

Don'ts

- Don't watch or listen to news programs at all if you are just a beginner. You shouldn't also do it too much if you already have some knowledge. It is a common trap people fall into while trying to practice and revise their Spanish vocabulary. The main purpose of these programs is to provide too much information within a short span of time. This is why these programs use lots of specific sentence structures and vocabulary.

Practice Your Vocabulary

Learning words and revising them is among the most crucial things when you want to practice your Spanish. This doesn't mean that you should always take a dictionary with you and revise every single word with translations. You can use special apps to help you practice Spanish and let you organize the process of word learning. This type of app works as the reminder for repeating words you learned the day before yesterday or yesterday. These apps determine how quickly you flip index cards and decide when to send a notification the next time it uses the information.

Be Patient

You have to keep in mind that when practicing Spanish, you won't be able to master the language overnight. You should remember that it needs lots of patience and efforts if you wish to get good and positive results.

If you ever find yourself stuck in a rut while learning Spanish, you can try to take a step back and review those things you already know. Maybe you missed something, and this is why you are having some problems right now.

Stay Motivated

Always remind yourself why you are doing what you are doing and what your ultimate goal is for all the work you have already done so far. You can also try praising yourself for the results you made but make sure you do not go overboard here. Such praises can ensure that you stay on the right track as you practice Spanish.

Don't Worry About Mistakes

Everyone makes mistakes, so never be afraid if you are wrong at times. These mistakes will help you learn how to do things right along the way.

It is not an easy walk in the park to learn a new language. But sooner or later, you will see your hard work's results and hear your first compliments, and you will be more proud of yourself like never before!

CONCLUSION

(CONCLUSIÓN)

Learning a second language is not that easy but you have to admit that it is challenging. Aside from your native language, it is quite challenging to learn about a very unfamiliar language like the Spanish Language. *(Aprender un segundo idioma no es tan fácil, pero debes admitir que es un desafío. Además de su idioma nativo, es bastante difícil aprender sobre un idioma muy desconocido como el español.)*

Here, you have learned the correct pronunciation of some Spanish words, the proper gestures that must accompany the statement that you are making, and also the use of verbs, pronouns, nouns, adjectives, adverbs, prepositions and the like. Through this tool, you have learned all grammatical factors without enrolling in a formal class-type review of Spanish Language. *(Aquí, ha aprendido la pronunciación correcta de algunas palabras en español, los gestos adecuados que deben acompañar a la declaración que está haciendo, y también el uso de verbos, pronombres, sustantivos, adjetivos, adverbios, preposiciones y similares. A través de esta herramienta, ha aprendido todos los factores gramaticales sin inscribirse en una revisión formal de clase de español.)*

Furthermore, there are also short stories which make the learning even more exciting. Through some tips in reading, you will surely find Spanish Language reading and learning enjoyable instead of considering it as a burden. *(Además, también hay historias cortas que hacen que el aprendizaje sea aún más emocionante. A través* de algunos consejos en lectura, seguramente encontrará agradable la lectura y el aprendizaje del idioma español en lugar de considerarlo como una carga.)

The use of short stories may be considered as designed for kids or children who are learning through baby steps, but the truth is that a learner of second language is considered as baby steps too. There is no harm in considering it as a kid-like way of learning. That is again a form of humility. Remember that humility is the start of learning. *(El uso de cuentos cortos puede considerarse diseñado para niños o niños que están aprendiendo a través de pequeños pasos, pero la verdad es que un aprendiz de segundo idioma también se considera como pequeños pasos. No hay daño en considerarlo como una forma de aprendizaje infantil. Esa es nuevamente una forma de humildad. Recuerda que la humildad es el comienzo del aprendizaje.)*

As parting words, you should always carve in your mind that learning is one way of showing humility because you are admitting into yourself that you still have a lot to learn and that will make you even more fit to perfect your goal – in this instance, the Spanish Language and Grammar. *(Como palabras de despedida, siempre debes recordar que aprender es una forma de mostrar humildad porque admites en ti mismo que todavía tienes mucho que aprender y que te hará aún más apto para perfeccionar tu objetivo; en este caso, Lengua y gramática española.)*

CPSIA information can be obtained
at www.ICGtesting.com
Printed in the USA
BVHW090455120521
607041BV00004B/937